PRAISE FOR *A FIELD GUIDE TO*

In *A Field Guide for Everyday Mission* Ben Connelly and Bob Roberts Jr. articulate the Christian mission and provide 101 helpful and practical steps to set about accomplishing this mission. This book will benefit small groups, individuals, and churches who are committed to reaching their communities for Christ.

ED STETZER, *President, LifeWay Research, and author,* **Subversive Kingdom**

Bob Roberts and Ben Connelly have given the local church an incredibly helpful and practical guide to doing mission that will equip everyone from the seasoned practitioner to the brand-new believer. It is simple and straightforward, yet it has the power to change both your neighborhood and the world for Christ.

MATT CARTER, *Pastor of Preaching and Vision, The Austin Stone Community Church, and coauthor,* **The Real Win**

Are you concerned about the state of the church in the West today? Are you affected by the need of the world around us? Do you struggle to know what you should do about it personally? This book will challenge you to become a missionary, right where you live, and not leave evangelism to the so-called professionals.

ADRIAN WARNOCK, *blogger and author,* **Raised with Christ**

If you find that "missional talk" can be a bit vague, then this is the book for you. It's an accessible guide to missional thinking. But even better, it will help put it into practice. It will show you what everyday mission can actually look like. Not every one of their 101 ideas will apply in your situation, but many of them will.

TIM CHESTER, *director, The Porterbrook Network, and author,* **A Meal with Jesus**

Ben and Bob do a phenomenal job creating a practical guide for missional living with a mix of story, theology, and simple, effective ideas to engage culture and do good. The world will be a better place as we begin to practice these ideas in our daily life rhythms.

CHRIS MARLOW, *founder and CEO, Help One Now*

I was always glad to support church missions but it took me many years to realize that I, too, had a mission. This very practical book helped me connect the dots in my understanding of that mission and offered me a way to step forward in faith. *A Field Guide for Everyday Mission* is written for all of us who wonder how to talk about and live out our faith in a natural, winsome, and God-honoring way.

DALE HANSON BOURKE, *author, The Skeptic's Guide series and* **Embracing Your Second Calling**

BEN CONNELLY
& BOB ROBERTS, JR.

A FIELD GUIDE
FOR EVERYDAY MISSION

30 DAYS AND 101 WAYS TO DEMONSTRATE THE GOSPEL

MOODY PUBLISHERS
CHICAGO

All Scripture quotations, unless otherwise indicated, are taken from *The Holy Bible, English Standard Version*. Copyright © 2000, 2001 by Crossway Bibles, a division of Good News Publishers. Used by permission. All rights reserved.

Edited by Elizabeth Cody Newenhuyse
Interior design: Design Corps
Cover design: Studio Gearbox
Cover image: Veer Image / #DVP4944378
Ben Connelly photo by Tina Howard-Fall Meadow Photography

Library of Congress Cataloging-in-Publication Data

Connelly, Ben (Pastor)
    A field guide for everyday mission : 30 days and 101 ways to demonstrate the gospel /
        Ben Connelly and Bob Roberts, Jr.
        pages cm
    Includes bibliographical references.
    ISBN 978-0-8024-1200-3
    1. Witness bearing (Christianity) 2. Apologetics. 3. Evangelistic work. 4. Missions. I.
    Title.
    BV4520.C6655 2014
    248'.5--dc23

                            2014007211

We hope you enjoy this book from Moody Publishers. Our goal is to provide high-quality, thought-provoking books and products that connect truth to your real needs and challenges. For more information on other books and products written and produced from a biblical perspective, go to www.moodypublishers.com or write to:

Moody Publishers
820 N. LaSalle Boulevard
Chicago, IL 60610

1 3 5 7 9 10 8 6 4 2

Printed in the United States of America

DEDICATION

BEN:
*To The City Church—This message is the drum we've beaten
since we started, and it's an honor that many of your stories
fill these pages. I love you and am grateful to demonstrate
the gospel with you.*

BOB:
*To NorthWood—As I have tried to teach you, you have taught
me more by how you engage on a daily basis glocally.*

CONTENTS

FOREWORD

Anyone who knows me knows will know that I tend to be a bit of a missional geek, a gatherer and synthesizer of ideas that collate around the missional task of the church in the twenty-first century. I've devoted much of my life to living missionally, developing our understanding of it in as many tribes of Christianity and on as many continents as I've been able. I believe it's the direction Christianity is going, and indeed is the direction it must go, if it's going to survive and thrive in increasingly post-Christian world. Developing a biblical missional theory, a viable strategy, as well as encouraging praxis has been the defining work of my life.

Following the thought line of James 2:17—that faith without works is dead—so also, a theory or a strategy without practice is dead. One can have the best missional theology, be the leading expert in missional theory, and be able to explain every missional structure and concept. But if one can't propel missional ideas out of their head and into their life, it doesn't matter. In that sense, *A Field Guide for Everyday Mission* is a valuable contribution to the missional conversation. This book fills a crucial gap, addressing some of the most common practical questions about missional life, in easy-to-follow answers. It's not an overly theoretical book, nor an academic one. It's not just for pastors and leaders; it's a helpful book for you: the everyday Christian, yearning to know how you can carry out God's call to hands-on mission in your already-too-busy, and yet oh-so-ordinary, life.

I have known Bob Roberts for years and have great love and respect for him. He has a proven track record of missional engagement, both locally and globally. From his extraordinary dedication and ongoing work in Vietnam, to getting to interact with well-known diplomats across the world, to training thousands of church planters over the past twenty years, Bob knows how to live a life on mission, and how to lead others to do the same.

Ben Connelly is a new voice in the missional conversation. But as a creative thinker, emerging leader, and innovative missional practitioner, Ben is living in the heart of a city helping others shape every aspect of their lives around Jesus and His mission. In other words, Bob has a proven and continuing ministry, and Ben represents a new generation of leader, adding insights to the development of the missional movement. Together, these men give us a glimpse of the future of missional work: they show you what mission can look like in your—yes, *even your!*—workplace, neighborhood, school, and home.

In this book Ben and Bob serve us by painting a clear picture of potentially confusing concepts. Exploring the six most basic questions of any inquiry—who, what, when, where, why, and how—they build a well-rounded image of one's life on mission: a worshipful understanding of our motivation, a deep knowledge of our mission fields, a helpful glimpse of life as a missionary, a tangible grasp of ways to reflect the gospel in our daily actions, and a variety of ways to share the gospel with our words.

In a meaningful mix of tradition and innovation, and of life in the Bible and life today, they draw each answer straight from Scripture, and do a good job contextualizing first-century, Middle Eastern, biblical practice to a twenty-first-century Western world. They share their own journeys toward living out God's mission as two ordinary Christian men, with some hits and misses along the way. They give further examples from the lives of everyday friends in their own cities, as well as from respected missional leaders in various contexts around the world. Each day's concept has a touch of theory that carries a hefty implicit biblical theology (especially for such small articles), as well as some hands-on ways to live out that day's idea. So in thirty bite-sized chunks, they share both biblical principles and implementable practices you'll need to pursue Jesus' Great Commission in your own life.

In that sense, this book truly is a "field guide." Let me encourage you: don't read it and forget it. Don't highlight sections and merely think, "That's a good idea," but do nothing about it. Instead, let Ben and Bob guide you through your own missional quandaries. Prayerfully consider their ideas. Use them as a starting point to get your own creative missionary juices flowing. Discuss them with others. Even tweak them for your unique mission field. And by all means, *DO* some of the things they recommend! Be bold and try them. And if you botch one or two (or all thirty!) of the days, thank God for grace, dust yourself off, and practice again.

That's my journey. But just like Ben, Bob, myself, and every other Christian in history, God has you on one of your own. You may be at the foothills of your journey, hesitant toward the daunting task in front of you. You may be at a fork in the road, confused by which way to go. You may be ready to throw in the towel. You may have the glorious summit of your trail in your sights and simply need a few pointers for those last precious meters. Or you may even be fighting the journey, doing your best to avoid it at all costs. But it's still upon you. Wherever you are on your unique missional journey, you hold in your hands a solid guide to help you with your next practical step. I trust you will take that step. The future of biblical Christianity in the West depends on it.

—*Alan Hirsch*

START HERE

FIVE QUESTIONS

"YOU'RE GOING TO TRY TO CONVERT ME, AREN'T YOU?"

That was Jerry's response to learning I was a Christian—and even a pastor.* Jerry is my office-mate at the local university where he and I teach communications classes. He is a fantastic, devout Jewish man. Although he *did* order bacon on his burger that day, as we enjoyed the patio of The Love Shack, a tasty burger joint you should try if you're ever in town. His story is one of a Jewish boy growing up in "Christian" Fort Worth, trying a few churches in his adult years, and being put off by attempt after attempt to convert him. He was ready to put down his non-kosher deliciousness and walk away from what he assumed would turn into another in a long line of evangelistic presentations. Before we could finish lunch, I had to assure him that my goal wasn't to "convert" him. I wanted to know him; to be his friend. I wanted to see him as a person, not a project. I even told him that my theology doesn't allow me to think I *could* convert him; *I* don't have that power. "But Jerry," I warned, "if God has other plans and does something through our friendship, you can't be mad at me, okay?" "He won't," Jerry said with an indignant laugh. And he stayed.

---

*Ben wrote the majority of the content for our book, which Bob invaluably spoke into, expanded, and edited. Most of the personal pronouns—like "I" or "my"—refer to Ben. When referencing Bob, he'll make that clear, with something like "I (Bob)" or "My (Bob's)."

Jerry is not alone in his perspective. He speaks on behalf of millions of people. Not just people across the world, but people who live next door to us; who go to work or school with us; who surround us every day. They've been burned by churches; they've been offended by Christians; they don't believe Jesus is the Messiah—yet.** But as Christians, *we do* follow Jesus; we've read the Bible; we know the "great commission" and even *want* to make disciples. At least sometimes. We have a God-given command and Spirit-empowered desire to share the gospel. But we have no idea how. It's offensive. It's divisive. It's just so hard!

But what if it didn't have to be so hard? What if the main reason we ignore mission isn't that the gospel is difficult and offensive (because it is)? What if the main reason we avoid talking about Jesus isn't that we view "missions" as an overseas-exclusive activity (because it isn't)? What if the main reason is that we simply don't know *how*? These are the questions we've both been wrestling with for the past several years.

OUR MISSIONS: BEN AND BOB

Bob and I are both pastors. We're both seminary-trained church planters. We love our churches. And we believe the Church is God's means of reflecting the gospel and making disciples. We had both worked in ministry for many years. We'd both even been, as they say, "successful." But at a different point in each of our lives, we were confronted with big questions about ministry and mission that neither of us knew how to answer.

For me, the big question came during grad school. Amidst the lectures and late nights of 2007, I lay awake asking, *If I was dropped on an island, with no prior knowledge of Christianity and nothing but the Bible as my guide, how would I live?* I became determined to contextualize the lifestyle, ministry, and mission of the first-century church, to twenty-first-century Texas. I found I wasn't alone. Christians

---

**Throughout the book, we use "not-yet-Christians" to refer to those who don't follow Jesus. We explain the two-sided intentionality in the book's conclusion ("End Here: Your Mission"), but if it bothers you enough to ruin the ending of the book now, flip to page 210.

were hungry to pursue ministry beyond the Church as they knew it, and not-yet-Christians were equally hungry to see Christians live out our faith in meaningful ways. Then we started The City Church in 2009, to live as "a family of disciples on mission," displaying and declaring our faith, and pursuing the mission of God, in the city where God sent us.

My (Bob's) story was a little reversed. I'd already started North-Wood Church when I became obsessed with the concept of the kingdom of God and its radical redefinition of God's expectations on His people. One of those expectations was going global. The question that plagued me was, *What if the church was a missionary?* In 1995, that question landed us in Hanoi, Vietnam, and some surrounding villages. Fast-forward to today: hundreds of American Christians have joined us in Vietnam. We've worked with orphans, universities, hospitals, artists, and the business community. After two decades, we even have strong relationships with the president, prime minister, and others. But the biggest missionary lesson we initially learned is that mission wasn't just for Vietnam. As people experienced life, ministry, and mission in a foreign city, they began to do the same things in our own.

Our journeys have led us both to view ourselves not just as pastors, but as missionaries. In addition to co-pastoring The City Church, I teach classes at TCU. That's officially Texas *Christian* University, but it's not. *Playboy* magazine recently ranked it the #9 party school in the nation, according to university news site TCU360.com.[1] I get to build relationships with colleagues (I use that term loosely, since they're all geniuses. I'm not) and students who would never walk into my church, Bob's, or any other.

And in addition to leading NorthWood, I (Bob) have found myself in politics, education, development, and transformation around the globe, meeting some of the most well-known—and even notorious—leaders of various faiths and nations. We intentionally go into the world around us and work secular jobs for the sake of living on everyday mission. And we strive to lead others to the same.

ARE YOU ASKING THE SAME QUESTIONS?

"Missional" is a sexy word in American Christianity today. Many Christians believe in missional theology; several understand missional theory; there are lots of missional resources for academics and leaders, to help lead others. But what about practical, everyday, immediately implementable advice? There's a point in every missional journey we each must ask, "How?" That's the #1 point of confusion, giving up, and for some, pull-out-your-hair-angst we've seen, as we've both led our churches and trained Christians across the country in everyday mission.

As we continue working through the messiness of mission in our own lives, we find more and more Christians asking the same kind of questions we were. "Can *even* I make disciples?" "What's it look like to share the gospel?" and "What are some ways to live out God's mission, in my crazy, busy, yet ordinary, mundane, everyday life?" If questions like these have crossed your mind, you're in luck: this is what we'll tackle in the coming pages.

"THE FIVE W'S": HOW TO USE THIS FIELD GUIDE

I teach in the Bob Schieffer College of Communication, named for the iconic broadcast journalist, one of TCU's most famous alums. Journalism schools teach students basic questions to ask when gathering facts for a news story. Most of us have known these questions since about first grade. We ask them every day, whether we attended a journalism school or not. Today they're called "the Five W's": Who? What? When? Where? Why? And then the curveball, sixth question: How? To understand the biblical, practical ins and outs of everyday mission, we have to answer these six questions. That's where we're going for the rest of the book:

→ Who is my everyday mission field?

→ What does an everyday missionary do?

→ When does everyday mission happen?

→ Where does everyday mission happen?

→ Why should I even care about everyday mission?

→ How do I share the gospel without killing the relationship?

You could read this alone, and you could read it like a normal book. If you did, some of you could finish it in a matter of hours. But each day is designed to be implemented in our lives and contexts, rather than just "checking it off" our overly full reading lists. So it's best if worked out alongside others who are wrestling with similar questions, and we suggest reading it over the course of six weeks. Spend the first five days each week considering daily answers to that week's question. Each day includes a biblical principle and examples and tips for living out the principle in ordinary life. The sixth day, get personal: answer that week's question and read one of our friends' stories, of that week's answers in their own everyday mission. The seventh day, meet up to discuss the week: share excitement and struggles; encourage each other's missions. And every day of each week, choose one of the 101 ways we suggest—or create your own—and practice, practice, practice.

WHAT WE AREN'T TRYING TO ACCOMPLISH

To vaccinate against the Plague of Assumption, we need to administer a few doses of Disclaimer:

1. We aren't against preaching, proclaiming the gospel, apologetics, evangelistic events, or even street preachers. We believe in, and have seen God use all those—and stranger— means to draw people to Himself. Instead, we're trying to inspire mission, even for those who never lead a church or own a soapbox. God doesn't just use the spectacular; He uses ordinary lives, activities, events, and relationships of *all* His people for His mission.

2. We aren't discounting the unique spiritual gift of evangelism. We praise God that clearly He gave some to be evangelists (Ephesians 4:11). This allows some of the events in #1 to come naturally to specific individuals. Instead, we're trying

to keep those *without* that gift from ignoring mission. Some Christians are given the gift of evangelism, but all Christians are given the mission of making disciples. We're helping those who are more scared than gifted, see that by the power of God, living on mission isn't as hard as we often think.

3. We don't separate "displaying" and "declaring" the gospel. One popular saying falsely encourages, "preach the gospel at all times. Use words if necessary."[2] Another says that mission is exclusively proclamation: if it doesn't involve a doorbell and question involving hell, it ain't mission. Both action and proclamation have their place in the mission of God. On one hand, by their very existence even "the heavens declare the glories of God" (Psalm 19:1) without a mouth to open; on the other hand, the gospel is a word and words must be spoken. The Bible calls us to both work and word; to both display *and* declare the gospel.

4. We aren't trying to create a legalistic blueprint to follow. If you're hoping these thirty days are "a guaranteed checklist for making five new Christians in a month or your money back," you'll be sorely disappointed. A, we won't refund you. B, that's not our goal. We're walking a fine line between being practical but not creating a system or method to follow. We're simply searching the scriptures, considering the biblical principles for everyday mission seen thousands of years ago, and transferring them to our everyday lives today.

WHAT WE ARE TRYING TO ACCOMPLISH

To those ends, what you hold in your hands is a field guide. It's written for you, the everyday Christian, trying to live out God's mission wherever God has placed you; you, the confused follower of Jesus asking how you possibly can live out that mission; you, the long-time believer who feels there must be something more. We wrestled through our questions; we hope to help with yours.

One final disclaimer: we write as imperfect examples trying to figure this out by God's grace. And by grace upon grace, we write as men who get to lead others to do the same, despite making plenty of mistakes along the way. Like just this week when I entered a coffee shop and asked the only guy sitting alone if he was the man I was supposed to meet: "Are you Christian?" I was confused by his unsure "uh, not really"—until I realized what he thought I'd asked. I stuttered out an apology, explaining that I was seeking a guy *named* Christian. Then we sat alone at separate tables for fifteen minutes, apparently having both been stood up. Then I left. *Way to seize the opportunity, Connelly.* And what happened with Jerry after that Love Shack burger? We'll tell you later—it's probably not what you think. For now, we just need to acknowledge before Day 1 that everyday mission is messy, and only exists by the grace of God, which works despite—and even through—our inadequacies, botched chances, and messes. Ready to jump into the grace-filled mess of everyday mission with us? Turn the page and let's go.

101 WAYS TO DEMONSTRATE THE GOSPEL

Each day ends with three or four ways to put these principles into practice.[3] But like every good demonstration, "showing" isn't enough; we must "tell" as well. So each day, consider . . .

→ . . . How Jesus changes our motives in these actions, which are otherwise done in goodwill

→ . . . What attribute of God, or fruit of the gospel is displayed (example: "generosity" or "grace")

→ . . . How each display of gospel fruit might become a chance to declare the gospel message

→ . . . New ways you'd add to our list, in your unique context. Share them online with the hashtag, #everydaymission and we'll repost in various ways

WHY SHOULD I EVEN CARE?

My daughters recently discovered *The Sound of Music*. Maggie is nearly two years old, and "dances," which consists of rocking side to side and spinning. But Charlotte—almost four—has memorized most of the songs. Her current favorite? "Let's start at the very beginning, a very good place to start . . ." If you've never seen the musical—which Charlotte and many Americans agree is a travesty—Julie Andrews and the von Trapp children sing, "When you read you begin with A—B—C [but] when you sing you begin with do—re—mi"1. Without a strong foundation, the rest of this Field Guide crumbles. So this week is our starting block; our foundation; our "do—re—mi."

Generally the "Five W" questions begin with "Who?" But throughout the New Testament, the apostle Paul always starts with the heart before he speaks to actions. He always addresses the "Why" before he gets practical. And we feel like he's a decent example to follow. So we begin by giving you five reasons to care about everyday mission. Each starts with God and the story He wrote from Genesis to Revelation, and continues to write, in and through each of our lives.

DAY 1

SURPRISE!
YOU'RE A MISSIONARY

LET'S PRETEND WE'VE NEVER HEARD OF JESUS.

ANSWER
We care because God saved us and gives us a new identity

READ
2 Corinthians 5:17–20

As you pretend with us, here's a question: *What defines you?* Here's my answer even if I didn't know Jesus: I am husband to Jess, father to Charlotte, Maggie, and God willing, more kid-dos in the future. I'm son to Dennis and Becky, a brother, brother-in-law, and uncle. And even if I (Bob) didn't know Jesus, I am husband to Niki and father to Ben (not my coauthor; a different one who looks like me) and Jill. I'm son to Bob Sr. and Gaye. I'm a brother, uncle, father-in-law, and nephew. And as of October 2013, I'm a granddad! We're both Americans, and we're both Texans. Yeehaw.

While these are marks of our identities, we both also play unique roles. Various titles describe us: we're both writers and speakers. Bob's a diplomat and resident of Keller. I'm a professor and resident of Fort Worth. We're both pastors (that's weird since we're pretending we don't know Jesus, right?). But while these titles *describe* us, and help direct where our time goes, they're not our *identity*. They're *roles* we play. They're meaningful, and we both hope to continue playing our roles for as long as God allows. But roles change. Neither of us lives where we grew up; we have both worked for multiple churches. So our residential and pastoral roles have changed.

Unlike roles, identities are permanent. Deeper than roles, our identity is who we are. There was a time when Bob and I were both single. There was a time when neither of us had children (those were the blessed days we could sleep past sunrise). But at specific moments, our identities objectively changed. We became husbands and dads, and now we live as married men with wives and children. These aren't hats we wear when we want and take off when we don't feel like living them out. They're more like tattoos that cannot be removed. Even if we could cover them up or they fade over time, once there, they're always there. If either of us is on a trip without our wives, neither gets to act as if we are single. Even as our kids grow and start families of their own, we're still parents. And when we're in Europe, we don't try to put on accents to fit in. We'd make fools of ourselves. I often tell my wife, Jess, that if I could change one thing about myself, I'd have a British accent—it just sounds so jolly cool. But because of who I am, I speak Texan, y'all.

What about you? If you didn't know Jesus, how would you define your identity? And what are some of the roles you play in your day-to-day life?

WHO WE ARE DEFINES WHAT WE DO

Okay, let's get back to loving Jesus. As we said, in nearly every one of Paul's New Testament letters, he explains "who you are" before he tells readers "what to do." He starts with our identity before he explains our roles and actions. "Christian" isn't just a role we play; it isn't just something we do. It's deeper than that. Our very *identity* is in Christ. Because of God's work in us, we are each sons and daughters of God. We are followers of Jesus. To take it a step further, that's a more important identity than "spouse," "parent," nationality or culture, or any way we define identity.

Before Jesus intervened in our lives, we were each, among other things, "a sinner . . . idolater . . . of our flesh . . . in darkness . . . slaves . . . children of wrath . . . [and] dead."[2] But in Christ, God has given us a new identity. We've been "transformed by the renewing of your minds"; God has removed the heart of stone from our flesh; we're now "children of light, a new creation . . . alive in Him."[3] Nearly every reference to salvation in the Bible speaks of a transfer of identities: we were *that*; by God's grace, we're now *this*.

That's the first reason we care about everyday mission. We have a new identity, and that new identity shapes our lives. God's gospel work doesn't stop at the moment of change. In fact, that new identity is just the beginning of God's work in and through us. Second Corinthians 5 explains our new identity, and reminds us that it's only through Jesus that this is possible. But Paul doesn't stop there. What else does God do? He "gave us the ministry of reconciliation." He entrusts us with his "message of reconciliation." He calls us His "ambassadors." Many Bible passages that speak of salvation echo the idea that our new identity calls us to demonstrate the gospel: in Romans, the gospel—"the power of God for salvation"—also enables us to live by faith; in Ephesians, the same God who saves us by grace, through faith also calls us "his workmanship, created in Christ Jesus for good works which God prepared beforehand, that we should walk in them."[4] Throughout most of the Bible, we see that our decisions, actions, and even roles stem from that new identity.

Our identity leads us to demonstrate the gospel. This isn't just true for the tiny percentage of Christians who actively choose to call themselves "missionaries," who get on a plane for the more traditional picture of "mission." It's true for everyone redeemed by God.

LIVING OUT OUR IDENTITY IN OUR ROLES

Gabe and Alison are actors in The City Church. They have helped me see the dangers of defining ourselves by the roles we play, instead of the identity we have. A professor once told Alison that any play worth watching is about an extraordinary day, be it triumph or tragedy. While that may be the formula for good entertainment, Alison explains the downside: "it fosters a false expectation of reality [for actors], leaving ordinary day to day seeming like no life at all."[5] Christian actors must cling to something deeper, something realer, as they rest in Christ and demonstrate the gospel in the dark world of professional theater. They can't be defined by critics' reviews, audiences' responses, or roles they play—because those change every few weeks. They live out their *identity* in Christ, in their roles as actors. This is true for every Christian, in every role we play. I'm paid to teach college freshmen about public speaking—or how to "talk good," I often joke. But I cannot ignore the fact that I am first a Christian, and God's missionary. I live out my identity *in* that specific role. I'm open about my faith from the first day of class. I get to know students. I try to model integrity, and to talk about Jesus when I can do so naturally. I seek to display grace and truth—which can be especially difficult when it comes to final exam grades!

Whatever we do in life, we are first and foremost disciples of God. We are members of His family. And we are missionaries to His world. It looks different depending on our place in life. But in whatever role we play—and even in lesser elements of our identity—we don't get to disregard to our deepest identity. We do business differently. How we treat others changes. The way we respond to frustration is redeemed. Our roles are renewed: they're each opportunities to live out our faith.

101 WAYS
TO DEMONSTRATE THE GOSPEL

1 Fix broken things: Jesus saw blindness and other disabilities as symbolic of spiritual brokenness; we can too. Pick up trash, paint fences, help a neighbor with rehab, or clean a park.

2 Be generous: Sacrifice your time, money, and resources for the good of others. This echoes the generosity, sacrifice, grace, and initiation God first showed you.

3 Back up your ministry with your message: Be aware how the work of the gospel is echoed in your cleaning, fixing, renewing, and serving. Be willing to explain this when asked.

THE GOOD NEWS OF JESUS IS BIGGER THAN YOU

If you were asked, "What is the gospel?" you'd probably speak of who God is, who He originally designed mankind to be, what sin did to distort our original purpose, and how Jesus is our only hope for eternity. And praise God—you'd be right! But the gospel doesn't just call us to God, to spend the rest of our lives as we please. God doesn't change our identity so that we can hide away from the world and wait for eternity. No! In our conversion, God changes our identity; our identity impacts our roles and changes our actions. The gospel is not *just* for the purpose of individual reconciliation; the gospel does not *just* call each of us out of our old identity. The gospel *also* calls us to participate in God's reconciliation of all things. The gospel *also* calls us to live out our new identity, every day as His ambassador. Why do we care about everyday mission? Surprise: by the fact that you call yourself a Christian, God calls you a missionary.

PAY IT FORWARD

DAY 2

WHAT HAPPENS IF ANIMALS STOP REPRODUCING?

If flowers stop producing pollen to spread? First endangerment, then if not reversed, extinction. I once met with an organization's leaders, who became increasingly uncomfortable through our conversation, as I encouraged them to equip their members toward God's mission. "It's just that" one finally said and paused, " . . . we're a more *inward-focused* organization." It's a popular label for Christian groups; it sounds good and holy. But Christianity is an outward-focused faith. From creation in Genesis, God designed every healthy, living organism to multiply: "plants . . . trees . . . winged birds . . . livestock and creeping things and beasts of the earth . . . [and] man" all "bear fruit . . . according to its kind"[6]. Healthy trees make new trees. Healthy duck-billed platypuses make new platypuses. Healthy humans make new humans. So do healthy Christians make new Christians.

God's Church is a living organism: multiplication and reproduction are not just physical, but spiritual. If we never multiply—if we never make disciples—we aren't healthy Christians.

But aren't community and discipleship good things? Yes. Growing together, carrying out the "one another" commands in Scripture, and

ANSWER
We care because God specifically sends us

READ
Matthew 28:16–20

building up the body are biblical concepts. Every plant and animal and human must mature—at least for a few days—before they multiply or reproduce. But *the gospel must spread*. We cannot live inward-focused lives if we claim to follow an outward-focused God.

AN OUTWARD-FOCUSED GOD;
AN OUTWARD-FOCUSED COMMISSION

Perhaps we don't live on mission because an "outward-focused God" is a new idea. Even if new to us, the concept is thousands of years old. Here are a few of Jesus' own words on the topic:[7]

- → "Those who are well have no need of a physician, but those who are sick."

- → "I tell you, there will be more joy in heaven over one sinner who repents than over ninety-nine righteous persons who need no repentance."

- → "For the Son of Man came to seek and to save the lost."

- → And even one of the most famous verses of the Bible: "For God so loved the world, that he gave his only Son, that whoever believes in him should not perish but have eternal life."

From God's promised Redeemer in Genesis to the culmination of that promise in Revelation, the Bible is a story of God's mission. And each of God's people between those points in history plays a vital role in that mission. Each of the four Gospels includes some form of Jesus' call to His followers, to make new disciples—most famously in Matthew 28. There has been a lot of debate over whether the Great Commission's "go" should be translated as a command ("go!") or participle ("as you go"). Honestly, God uses His people in both ways: some leave home on mission to a new place (like Abraham, Jim Elliot to South America, St. Patrick to Ireland, and the apostle Paul to, well, most of the Roman Empire). Others (like Israel's prophets, George Müller with British orphans, Jesus' brother James, and Jesus Himself) made disciples where they lived.

While the second view is the topic of this book, debating the nu-anced Greek wording might miss the forest for the leaves on the trees. The kingdom of God might be better served if we just live out the explicit command in the verse: "make disciples of all nations." Both our own and the other 195 across the globe,[8] wherever God sends us. Bigger than the translating "go" is the question, *Are you making disciples?* Whoever you are; wherever you're called, are you pursuing God's mission?

Early in my (Bob's) ministry, my primitive understanding ac-tually got in the way of Jesus' teaching in the Great Commission. I remember once giving a call in our worship gathering to anyone who felt called to be a missionary. But Jesus had already given the call to everyone. My job was not to issue the call but to show people their call and equip them fulfill it. For many, the call wasn't about seminary, preaching, cross-cultural involvement, or religious work; it was about everyday discipleship in every way, engaging society by using what God had given, to bless others.

PAY IT FORWARD

The 2000 film *Pay It Forward*[9] re-popularized a concept first coined in 1919, of doing good deeds to others in response to first receiving a good deed. Haley Joel Osment's eleven-year-old Trevor McKinley's school project launches a citywide movement of do-goodery. Without asking his mom, he invites a homeless man to live with his family. Bad idea, Trevor. It turns out okay: the man "pays forward" the favor by doing chores around the house, and later stops someone else's suicide attempt. Grateful for life, that person pays it forward again. And so forth. The past century has seen many versions of this concept. Attempts often lean toward moralistic, feel-good motives, temporary justice, and even overtones of karma. But it is a helpful picture of God's mission: He sends us to make dis-ciples, as He first sent someone to make a disciple of us, and some-one else made a disciple of them, and so forth. With better records, each Christian on earth could trace our spiritual family to the eleven apostles (or later, Paul) who heard Jesus' original commission, "Go make disciples."

Spoiler alert—if you don't want to ruin a decent movie, skip to the next paragraph. But there's a massive difference between *Pay It Forward* and the Great Commission. After seeing this movement spread through his city and beyond, Trevor dies—ironically while trying to do good. In a pseudo-Christlike ending, the hundreds impacted by the movement he started show up to a vigil, each committing to keep it alive. Less-Christlike, however, is that Trevor stays dead. So the continuation of his revolution relies completely on his followers. That's *not* how God works in His mission.

Remember what I told Jerry in the introduction? "My theology doesn't allow me to believe I can convert people." That's biblical honesty. I don't have the power, words, winsomeness, ability, or at times, even desire to make disciples. Even the most gifted evangelist cannot carry out the Great Commission by their own power. God alone convicts, changes hearts, leads to repentance, reveals idols, and draws people to Himself. This is why the end of verse 20, often less quoted than verse 19, is vital: "And behold, I am with you always, to the end of the age." We'll dive deeper into God's power

101 WAYS TO DEMONSTRATE THE GOSPEL

4 Build relationships: Stories get deeper, trust is built, and needs are expressed, only as relationships get stronger. Make time, ask questions, and visit often. Share your story and remember as they share theirs.

5 Take—or teach—a class or lessons: do adult education, cooking, fitness, art, or whatever you're passionate about. If there's no class offered in an area of your skill or passion, start one.

6 Don't forgo Christian practices in not-yet-believers' presence: Speak truth. Encourage, exhort, or rebuke others in love, as you normally would. Pray. Take communion. Demonstrate the difference your faith makes.

in the coming weeks. For now, God both commands and causes His Commission.

Why care about everyday mission? Because the Bible is the story of a sending Father, who sent His Son to "seek and save the lost."[10] Because God sent someone to "seek and save" you, and you are now part of a sent people. Just as He commands and causes plants, animals, and humans to reproduce, He commands and causes disciples to be made in our lives. We are the vessels He chose to pay His mission forward. But we must embrace the commission God has put on every one of His people: when God asks "Whom shall I send, and who will go for us?" our understanding of a sending God and the Great Commission drives us to respond like Isaiah, "Here I am! Send me."[11]

DAY 3

PITFALLS AND TRAPS

ANY GOOD FIELD GUIDE GUARDS YOU FROM DANGERS ON THE TRAIL.

Today, we play spiritual doctor and examine our hearts and heads, diagnosing pitfalls and traps in our minds, which can derail our everyday mission. Pitfalls are lies we believe, which *keep some of us* from making disciples. Traps, on the other hand, *drive some of us* to try to make disciples, but in unhealthy—even ungodly—ways. Once we discover these powerful dangers in our hearts, we can pinpoint the only treatment for both.

PITFALLS THAT KEEP OUR MOUTHS SHUT

When Jesus sent His first disciples into mission, "he said to them, 'Take nothing for your journey, no staff, nor bag, nor bread, nor money; and do not have two tunics. And whatever house you enter, stay there, and from there depart.'"[12] The first Christian missionaries had no choice but to meet people wherever they went: if they didn't, they'd have been hungry and homeless. Maybe we would meet people better if our lives—or at least a hot meal and good night sleep—depended on it. Today, politeness, introversion, and shyness are common reasons some Christians don't pursue mission. Each often gets slammed as being bad or wrong, but while we guard you from the lie—"I can't live on mission because of my personality"—we also want to

ANSWER
We care because mission is an act of worship

READ
Romans 11:33–12:2

free you to live on mission in your unique gifting, instead of telling you to overcome or change it.

Politeness

Politeness is good. The Bible celebrates those who consider others more highly than themselves.[13] In fact, one reason many not-yet-believers dislike Christians is our *lack* of politeness. Politeness becomes a pitfall, though, when it slips into people-pleasing—the "fear of man."[14] When we make excuses against knocking on a neighbor's door, convince ourselves of reasons not to talk to the new guy at work, and tell ourselves we're a bother, politeness hinders us. Our mission meets the same demise as the teenage boy who never works up the nerve to ask out the pretty girl. But a healthy level of politeness in an everyday missionary is a blessing. As we're honoring, respectful, and polite in our interactions, we build bridges instead of burn them. Politeness benefits mission.

Introversion

At least a third of the US population is introverted.[15] So if mission can only take place with lots of people, by extroverts who love being around all those people, God's mission is over 33 percent sunk! But introverts make great missionaries. You're generally thoughtful, and while you may have fewer conversations than extroverts, those you do have are often deep. You likely listen well. This makes you a stellar missionary. An introverted friend is a wine expert. When he overcame the misplaced shame of not pursuing lots of relationships, he began inviting one person or couple at a time to join him and his wife for homemade dinners and wine tastings. Tastings last for hours and involve lots of talking. His hobby and personality make him an intentional listener, thoughtful speaker, and engaging friend. God has borne fruit through his efforts, one person at a time.

Shyness

Distinct from introversion, many people consider themselves shy. Striking up a conversation is simply something several of us aren't comfortable with. John Mark is in my City Group, and was once relieved to be on "dinner duty" the night a new couple walked in. He was able to stay in the kitchen instead of interacting immediately. John Mark can still live on mission; he just finds it helpful to discover a point of connection, like a common interest or shared acquaintance. Something to focus on—a TV or project—eases his pressure. And for many, mission in community (see Day 21) is essential: others have initial conversations, while you listen and grow in comfort and relationship to the point you can engage.

If you're introverted, shy, or both, be relieved: yes Christians are called to make disciples, but we are never given a quota or a step-by-step guide of how. Introverts, go make *a* disciple! One at a time if that's what it takes. Shy? Take your time, and give yourself grace. Polite? That's great news; just make sure you fear God more than man. And as you work though all three pitfalls, do two things: pray for ideas, boldness, and open doors—just like extroverts and less-shy missionaries must do. And praise God for the strength to obey Him in the way He's designed and gifted you.

TRAPS THAT SHOULD KEEP OUR MOUTHS SHUT

While pitfalls keep us from everyday mission, Bob and I have both stood by the door after missions conferences as attendees excitedly exit. Many are on fire for God's mission—but for all the wrong reasons. Here are five traps people easily fall into, as we wrongly pursue everyday mission:

Duty

Nearly every job requires tasks we don't like. We all attend events out of obligation. Everyone does things because we have to. But we can't view mission through that lens. The prophet Jonah is often celebrated for finally going to Nineveh. But read the final two chapters of his story, and you'll find that he may not be as excited as many have come to think. Jonah goes only one-third of the way into the city to which he was sent; he pronounces judgment with no call to repent. And when God saves Nineveh anyway, Jonah sulks—*because* God saved them! Yes, Jonah went. But not happily, and he only did the bare minimum. The book ends as God rebukes Jonah's poor view of his mission.[16] Mission can't be a "just enough" pursuit, an empty obligation. Do you live on mission only because you have to?

Earning

From televangelists to Islam to some Catholicism, many religious traditions are largely founded on earning or losing favor: "If I don't do this, God won't do that . . . If only I'd do this, I'll be blessed like that . . ." In this trap, mission becomes an attempt to earn something from God or prove something to Him. But mission is not atonement. No number of conversions makes up for whatever darkness drives us; only Jesus overcomes our past. Likewise, mission cannot be a way to please God or avoid some punishment; only Jesus takes God's anger. Do you pursue mission to prove or earn something, before God or man?

Self-glory

Competition can be healthy—even fun. But sadly, we know people whose ministries, and even self-worth, are built on "how many people I've saved" compared to how many "you have." The obvious issue in this view is that souls are worth far more than notches on a belt! Deeper though, this puts ourselves in the place of God. Yes, He gifts some as evangelists—praise Him for it. But as He reminds Jonah, and echoes throughout the Bible, "Salvation belongs to the Lord.'"[17] We aren't responsible for the success of His mission, so we can't use His mission to build ourselves up. Do you do God's mission to promote yourself?

Doing "Good" Things

Mission is not truly mission if it doesn't involve Jesus. "Empty moralism" is doing nice things for people. It makes us feel good, and even benefits them for a time. But moralism alone stops short of mission: it doesn't require or point to Jesus, it lacks eternal impact, and it often stems from poor motives. Jesus celebrates the feeding and clothing of people in need. But people who don't know Jesus do that too. The final question of this book—"HOW do I share the gospel . . . ?"—helps us ensure movement from moralism to mission. We must *both* display the gospel by our actions *and* declare it by our words. Does your "mission" point people to Jesus, or just do nice things for others to feel good about yourself?

Trendiness

As we've said, "missional" is a sexy word right now. Some call it a trend. But as AOL Instant Messenger and the clothes in your parents' wedding photo prove, trends die off: As a word, "missional" may be a trend, but everyday mission is not. God's mission is as old as history, as broad as every inch of land on which a follower of Jesus stands, and as necessary to life in Christ as discipleship or community. We'll see practical ways to live on mission in the coming weeks, but we'll first show the gospel motive that undergirds everything we write. Do you pursue mission just because you think it's cool right now?

Why is each of these a trap? It's a question of motives. Are we focused on God or on us? Sneakily, the outward expression often looks the same, regardless of what drives us. And we all know the deceit of our hearts. We must be careful with motivation: mission must find its root in God and His gospel work in us, for the sake of His gospel work in our everyday mission fields.

THE BETTER PATH IN A YELLOW WOOD

If our pursuit of everyday mission has gone off the beaten path into pitfalls or traps, we may need to pray for boldness, or to repent of selfish motives. Like everything under the sun, God can redeem our fears, excuses, and poor motives. But today's point isn't to leave us hopeless about our souls. Instead, these pitfalls and traps show our need to find the right path. So we end today asking, "What is a *right* motive for everyday mission?" There is only one: mission is an act of worship.

Worship goes beyond songs and sermons. It involves pursuing obedience to God's commands. Even the hard ones. In today's reading, Paul reminds us that "all things"—including God's work in our own lives, the mission on which He sent us, and the gifting He's given each of us—are *from* God, provided *through* God. "All things" are also *to* God, for His glory. God is the beginning and end of His

101 WAYS
TO DEMONSTRATE THE GOSPEL

7 Foster or adopt a child: Reflect God's adoption of you by bringing someone out of a poor situation and into your family. Or financially, emotionally, and practically help a friend as they do the same.

8 Support international orphan prevention: Organizations are now working to keep children in their homes and cultures, and help them from becoming orphans by reconciling brokenness in families that would eventually put them on the streets.

9 Consider your week: How much are you alone? With other Christians? With not-yet-believers? If the last group gets the least time, leave your home, be outside more, invite them in... how can you look outward?

mission. God's work is both our motivator and goal. God's glory is the sole reason we obey God. What does obedience look like? Paul tells us in the very next verse: sacrifice. Sacrificial lives move past pitfalls and break out of traps, as God corrects our motivation. Sacrificial lives are lives of worship. God has uniquely prepared you for your place in it, has given you the only pure motive, and has shown you the only right goal. "So, whether you eat or drink, or whatever you do, do all to the glory of God."[18]

THE GLORY OF . . . SOMETHING

WHEN YOU THINK OF THE WORD "PRIEST," WHAT IMAGES COME TO MIND?

Black shirts with white collars? Flowing robes hanging on elderly shoulders? Seemingly ongoing news reports might bring a darker image to mind. Or maybe, if you've spent much time in the book of Leviticus—and of course, who hasn't?—you think of the Old Testament priesthood.

OLD AND NEW COVENANT PRIESTHOODS

In God's old covenant people Israel, He established a tribe of priests: beginning with Moses' brother Aaron, these "Levites"—as they were eventually known—mediated between God and man. They brought requests to God on behalf of His people; they prayed to God on behalf of His nation. They brought God's word to Israel, and they made animal sacrifices on Israel's behalf. Lots of animal sacrifices. Leviticus opens by describing Israel's many offerings, each symbolic of God's acceptance and forgiveness of His people and their sin. While the burden of bringing the offering was on each individual the priest carried out the sacrifice.[19] A far cry from our image of starched clerical collars, priests were often a blood-covered mess. And they were an essential point of connection between God and man.

ANSWER
We care because we all praise something— and only God is worth it

READ
1 Peter 2:9–12

But the descendants of Levi weren't God's only priests in the Old Testament. Before God set apart the Levites, and even before He gave Moses the Ten Commandments, He established His first human mediators: "Thus you shall say to the house of Jacob, and tell *the people of Israel*: You yourselves have seen what I did to the Egyptians, and how I bore you on eagles' wings and brought you to myself. Now therefore, if you will indeed obey my voice and keep my covenant, you shall be my treasured possession among all peoples, for all the earth is mine; *and you shall be to me a kingdom of priests and a holy nation*. These are the words that you shall speak to the people of Israel."[20] The entire *nation* of Israel, set apart and called by God, was to be a collective kingdom of His priests. It was the role of *all* of God's people to represent God not only to each other, but to the surrounding nations of the world.

Centuries after God calls His old covenant people "priests," He applies the same term to His new covenant people. In 1 Peter 2, God gives the same title to the Church as He did Israel. Now *we* are His priesthood, nation, and people. So again, when you think of the word "priest," what images come to mind? Go look in a mirror: if you are Christian, the picture of a priest is a picture of you.

No, God isn't asking us to set up a confessional booth or ball of incense. And thankfully, He doesn't ask us to burn any cows. Following the old covenant image, our role is to represent God to others. As Peter puts it, we "proclaim the excellencies of him who called you out of darkness into his marvelous light" to those around us. We care about everyday mission because the God who called us to Himself—likely through the words and work of His other new covenant priests—now calls us to His priesthood, to declare and display Him to the people He's sent us to.

WHAT DO YOU DECLARE THE EXCELLENCIES OF?

You already function as a priest of *something*. Every person on earth—Christian or not—"proclaim[s] the excellencies" of something or someone. In every decision we make, and by the things we do and in many words we say, we introduce people to the things that are most important to us. Even if subconsciously, the things that are the most important to us are the things we often look to be our gods. They're not likely little statues, but they are idols nonetheless. We'd rarely call them gods; some readers will likely even defend against us referring to them as such. But if we look to anything to satisfy us more than God—who has promised us His provision and goodness—we put that thing in God's place. If we seek anyone's approval above God's—who has already approved of us in the death and resurrection of Jesus—we make that person our idol. If hope, joy, meaning, or purpose comes from anyone or anything more than God, then on some level that thing functions as our god. Whatever we look to, to "make things right again"—in any given situation, that person or thing becomes our functional redeemer instead of Jesus.

What do you talk about most? What do you tweet about often? Whose pictures fill your frames and phone? What does your happiness and sadness rely on? These are twenty-first-century ways we proclaim the glory of something. Or where do you put your hope? What defines success to you? Whose opinions do you both fear and seek to please most? Don't these determine the choices you make, and the glory you functionally declare?[21]

If a Christian college senior's overarching goal is the highest-paying career, money or comfort might be a functional god. It

101 WAYS TO DEMONSTRATE THE GOSPEL

10 Look at your social media: Intentionally talk or tweet about Him, as much as you do the other things you enjoy and talk about, but would claim are less important than Him.

11 Interact online with grace: Few people are swayed by a social media rant or angry blog post. If you're social on social media, display grace and truth in your tone and comments.

12 Perform an "idol check": Where do your time, money, and other resources go? What do you think about in your free time? Are those false gods/functional saviors?

becomes the driving—or only—basis for choosing his first job, over relationships, work-life balance, or even God's calling. If the only hope for a single lady is a husband, the idea of marriage is her functional redeemer. And she might change her appearance, values, happy-hour hangout or church to pursue her god. If our joy rises and falls on how well our favorite team does, or if we constantly talk about a band, political party, philosophy, or body type, that may be our functional god. We declare the praise of these things every day through the things we do and say. Even if we don't realize it; even if we deny it; even if those things let us down, over and over again, we're all priests of something. The question is, *priests of what*?

A BETTER MISSION

We have bad news and good news, fellow modern-day priests. The bad news is that our political party *will* lose or let us down. The band we love *will* one day break up (even if it's only to reunite for publicity's sake). Our perfect bodies *will* give way to age and fat. We both know that one all too well: I recently had spinal surgery, and Bob got both a shiny new knee and hip last year. We *will* find a flaw in that supposedly perfect job. But the good news is that there's a better God to be a priest of: Jesus won't let us down. The author of Hebrews calls Jesus the only perfect Priest and Mediator, who effectively approached God on behalf of the world. Jesus is the one perfect Sacrifice, who lay down His life for us and frees us from everything that lets us down. In Jesus, we now get to live as a priest of the one thing that will never let us down.

If you're reading this and you don't know Jesus, you're *already* a priest, and you *already* declare excellencies of something—it's just of a false god that will let you down. Jesus came, lived, died, and rose so you can trade up to a better God and a better story. If you're reading this and claim to know Jesus, you too are *already* a priest, and you *already* declare excellencies—of something. And the only God in the universe that won't let you down called you to Himself and made you a priest of *Himself*. So now you can—and must—declare *His* excellencies to those around you, and in turn call others to the greatest story and mission imaginable.

MOVE OR SENT?

WHAT DO YOU DO NEXT?

After six hours paddling down the Amazon and what feels like six hundred mosquito bites, you've arrived. You're part of a missionary team sent to live with a tribe in the middle of the rain forest for the next decade. You tie your dugout canoe to a tree, and your translator asks around for your local contact. You meet him, then get settled into your five-foot-diameter hut.

What do you do next?

You walk out your front door, like you do every day, head to the car, get in and start driving to work. You give an obligatory wave to your neighbor, whose name is either Jim or John; you're never quite sure which. You work hard all morning. You eat a quick lunch at your desk alone, then back to the grind. You get home, mow the lawn, eat dinner, and watch TV until you drift off to sleep.

What do you do next?

MISSIONARIES AT HOME

We'd probably approach the first scene above with more missional intentionality, because that's more of the scenario we picture when we think of a missionary. But objectively, the second is no different: we each live in a city on planet Earth just like "traditional" missionaries do. That city is filled with neighbors, coworkers,

ANSWER
We care because God alone sent us to our mission fields

READ
Jeremiah
29:3–11

classmates, and friends who need Jesus, just like other missionaries' cities. And we were sent to our city by God, for the same purpose as the missionaries in the first scene. If we're honest about the second scene, "what we'd do next" is pretty much the same thing we did yesterday, and what we'll do tomorrow. We'd work the daily grind and wait for Saturday when we can relax and hit the beach or bike trails. We live in a context where everyday routine, comfort, and convenience can distract us from our missionary calling.

Just like God sends people to the Amazon or Asia or anywhere else in the world, He sent *you* into your city. Maybe it wasn't a canoe or plane that got you to your mission field. It was more likely a U-Haul or a buddy's pickup. Maybe you thought you were moving there for four years of college. Maybe a job transferred you there, or a promotion took you there. Maybe you met an attractive guy or gal who lived there and that's why you "coincidentally" ended up there. Maybe—just maybe—you were even captured during a war, caged up, and exiled to your current city.

GOD ALONE PUTS HIS PEOPLE WHERE HE WANTS THEM

Being exiled for the sake of mission might seem unlikely, but that was the case for ancient Israel. The army of Babylonian king Nebuchadnezzar had taken some of God's people captive into Babylon. Before we describe the scene, it's worth noting that in Jeremiah 29, God specifically says it wasn't Babylon's strength that took the Israelites into exile. It wasn't Israel's weakness that led them in captivity. It wasn't accident or even a lack of fighting well. God claims twice in these verses, "It was I who sent you there." And just before the verse that gets embroidered and hung on walls about God knowing plans He has for welfare, future, and hope, God declares that it was *His* intention to leave the exiles in Babylon for seventy years. This whole "exile thing" was God's plan.

That may be easy for us to stomach 3,000 years removed. But let's put ourselves in their sandals: what would we do if we ended up a prisoner in a different country? What would our mindset be toward those who raided our city, and likely did bad things to our relatives and burnt down our house as they took us away? Bob and I know our ungodly gut response: we'd likely do everything we could to get the heck out. To pray for deliverance. And we would certainly pray unmentionable things for our captors. But God had different plans for the folks He sent to Babylon: "Seek the welfare of the city where I have sent you into exile, and pray to the Lord on its behalf." These God-fearing exiles had a job to do; they had a purpose to carry out. They were literally sent into Babylon to live on mission there. Gardens weren't backyard plots with a few tomatoes and berries. God intended them to plant vast fields of crops to sell and trade. His call was to invest in the economic and social processes, build houses, and live their everyday lives amongst the Babylonians. Most difficult to swallow, He even commanded them to give their kids in marriage to the kids of the folks who captured them. All of these are ways to bless and impact their mission field. From a human mindset, this looks crazy.

OUR HOME, OUR MISSION

But that's our job too: we've been sent into—wherever we currently live—to live on mission there! College, a job, or a guy or gal? Like planes, trains, and automobiles, these things are just tools that God might have used to get you to your mission field. I grew up outside Fort Worth, but never thought I'd return. I love adventure, cool weather, mountains, and outdoor activities that cool weather and mountains provide. Fort Worth is hot and flat, and after a few minutes outside in August, you're likely dead. So at every juncture of life I tried to get to Colorado, to fulfill many Texans' dream of living in the glorious Rockies. But circumstances (or sovereignty) always kept me from realizing that dream. Four circumstances landed me in Fort Worth after college: a job offer, a scholarship to grad school in Dallas, a free place to live, and most importantly, the appeal of living in the same state as the girl who would later become my wife, who was finishing college in Waco. I stayed.

Over a decade later, after the humble honor of seeing Jesus move in many ways that wouldn't have been possible from the mountains, my family is committed to Fort Worth for life, barring a R-O-C-K-I-E-S-shaped cloud formation. Maybe you haven't yet fallen in love with your city or neighborhood. But if the image in Jeremiah most closely applies to modern refugees or asylum seekers, then where does that leave the rest of us, who more voluntarily ended up wherever we live? If even God's exiles were called to love the city God put them in, you and I have absolutely no excuse not to.

The hardest element of life in The City Church is sending people out of one neighborhood-based community—called City Groups—to live on mission together in their own neighborhood or in a different part of town. But sending is vital for City Groups. A willingness to pursue mission must exist if we're a *missional* community! We started our church with four groups; now in our fourth year, those have multiplied to over twenty. Many include people who only became involved in a church—and by God's grace some who have become believers—only because a City Group lives on mission on their block. If we believe God sent us to the place we live, we see that place through new eyes. City Groups grieve the loss of closeness and sacrifice, but celebrate God's work and send.

So look outside. Who do you see? What are their names? What do they do? What do they love? If you don't love your city (where God

101 WAYS
TO DEMONSTRATE THE GOSPEL

13 Be involved in your city: Serve your councilperson, or be a volunteer firefighter. Even consider running for your city council or school board.

14 Join your neighborhood association or local boards: These exist to serve, beautify, build relationships in, and fight for your neighborhood.

15 Don't just join these groups; get involved: Step into leadership, and help organize and influence the direction of your neighborhood or city. If these don't exist, be proactive and help create them!

has sent you)—or start smaller: if you don't love the neighbors on your block (who are broken but created in God's image)—why not? Astoundingly, like the talents in Jesus' parable,[22] God our Master entrusts us with His mission. We get the honor of reaping where others have sown; we have the chance to participate in seeing God produce fruit.

We pray that God opens our eyes to see that wherever we live— apartment, condo, house, couch in your office that your boss doesn't know you sleep on—is a location given by God. Or, to say it like Jesus did, "Look, I tell you, lift up your eyes, and see that the fields are white for harvest."[23] We didn't *actually* move here for a job, a guy or gal, or for any other reason. God sent us here. And God entrusts us with His work. We have a job to do. So again, *what do you do next?*

"WHY" QUESTIONS FOR YOU TO WORK THROUGH

☐ **GENERAL:** What impacted you the most this week? What was new, convicting, or confusing? What was difficult? What do you need to discuss with others?

☐ **GENERAL:** On a scale of 1–5, where would you currently rank your-self as an "everyday missionary"? (let's say 1 is "I'm horrible" and 5 is "the apostle Paul's got nothing on me").

☐ **DAY 1:** What are some of the words/titles God gives through the Bible, which speak to your new identity? Especially focus on those that echo of our identity as His missionaries.

☐ **DAY 1:** What are some of the roles you play in everyday life? What are some ways you can live out your missionary identity in some of those roles? Why is it difficult to do that?

☐ **DAY 2:** How does it impact your view of life, God, and mission, to know that God is a sending God, and that Christianity is an outward-focused faith?

☐ **DAY 2**: Who did God use to lead you to Jesus? If possible, can you find out who led them to Jesus, and so on? Who do you regularly interact with, who God might call you to lead to Himself?

☐ **DAY 3**: Which pitfalls or traps do you most naturally fall into? Others we didn't list? Why? How can God and others pull you out and set you on the right path for His mission?

☐ **DAY 3**: How are mission and the everyday activities of life acts of worship to God? Talk about specific ways these things bring glory to God.

☐ **DAY 4**: If priests are mediators between God and people, what does it mean that all of God's people through history—including you—are "a kingdom of priests"?

☐ **DAY 4**: What are some things you talk and tweet about, spend time and money on, and think about most? In what ways do you look to those things, to do what God promises to do? What are some ways they let you down?

☐ **DAY 5**: What did God use to bring you to the place you currently live?

☐ **DAY 5**: If God puts His people where He wants them, then what "spheres of influence" has He sent you to, as His missionary to those people? How have you done with His call to mission there?

☐ **GENERAL**: Look back over this week's "Everyday Mission Ideas." What additional, practical things can you come up with, specific to your personality, gifting, and mission field, to live out God's mission? Share your ideas online with the hashtag #everydaymission.

MY MISSION
LANCE FORD

KANSAS CITY, MISSOURI

Making the word flesh is the sweet spot of living on mission. For my wife and me, that concept means we take Jesus as literally as possible. So when Jesus says, "Love your neighbor as yourself," He means to love your actual neighbors. When He says, "Don't just throw a banquet and invite all your well-to-do friends, but invite the lonely and outcasts," what if He really means it?

Shortly after moving to Kansas City we learned of an eccentric neighbor in the house behind us. A few of the other neighbors called him "Crazy Dan." When I asked why, I was told he was just a mean old guy who lived as a hermit. The grounds around his house were overgrown and his house was beyond disrepair. My first glimpse of Dan seemed to confirm the word on the street. He looked not only crazy but a bit scary too.

I knocked on his door a few times, to introduce myself as his new neighbor. He never answered. Finally, one afternoon he drove past our house and I walked around to meet him. When I approached his car (which he was still sitting in), I waved and he rolled the window down. "What do you want?" Those were Dan's first words to me, ever. I introduced myself and told him I just wanted to meet one of my neighbors. He opened the car door and the smell hit me like a Mack truck. His car was filled with leftover fast, food wrappers and containers, and was altogether filthy. Other than the trash, the only thing in his car was his walker. Dan could only get around with the aid of his walker, which lay on the fast food mound. He was unshaven and unkempt, sitting in his car eating fast food. It was obvious that this was the way he took all his meals—alone from a drive-through window.

I knelt next to his car and we began talking. Within a few short minutes it was clear that Dan was not crazy. In fact, he was extremely intelligent. He had been a computer scientist when computers were not held on laps but filled huge laboratories. He was amazingly well read and on top of the latest news and political issues. He had insight and perspectives that went way below the surface, to the root of issues. He blew my mind with his ideas on how things could be better in society. No, Dan was not crazy. He was lonely. An hour after introducing myself I told him I had to get back home. Although I had only told him my name once—quickly after his gruff greeting when I wasn't sure he even heard me—he said, "I really enjoyed our visit, Lance. Come over anytime."

Thanksgiving and Christmas rolled around not long after meeting Dan, and we invited him to join our family for dinner on both occasions. He accepted both invitations and made the arduous journey, shuffling from his house to ours, and up two sets of steep steps into our home.

This story doesn't end with me leading Dan to Jesus. Not yet anyway. I may not be here for Dan as much as he is here for me. Jesus said how we act toward the "least of these" is how we act toward Him. The only thing I am sure of this every time I visit with Dan I feel that I have spent some time with Jesus, and that Jesus Himself is my neighbor, embodied by "not-so-crazy" Dan.

LANCE FORD serves on the National Leadership Team for Forge America Missional Training Network. He is a writer, coach, consultant, and cofounder of the Sentralized Conference, who has designed unique training systems currently being used by networks, seminaries, and leaders throughout the world. forgeamerica.com

WHO IS MY EVERYDAY MISSION FIELD?

"Africa!" two or three voices rang out. Then it was silent. I had just asked a couple hundred folks in a Sunday church service, "What do you think of when you think of missions?" "Africa!" was the lone response. "Can anyone think of anything else?" More silence. According to the church where I was invited to speak, "Missions = Africa." Exclusively. Surely there's more . . .

This week we ask, "WHO is my everyday mission field?" While the Bible gives many terms and examples, our regular mission primarily involves two groups of people: those in need and our neighbors. Jesus' brother James sums up both well. First, "Religion that is pure and undefiled before God, the Father, is this: to visit orphans and widows in their affliction, and to keep oneself unstained from the world." And a few verses later he says, "If you really fulfill the royal law according to the Scripture, 'You shall love your neighbor as yourself,' you are doing well."[1]

Many Christians have an easier time with one or the other, so we'll pursue neighbors at the expense of those in need, or those in need at the expense of neighbors. Or we'll pursue global mission at the expense of either side of local mission. Or if we're honest, some of us are uncomfortable with mission altogether, so we pursue none of the above.

God does not make these distinctions. The same God who commands us to go across the globe also commands, in the same verse, engaging our current city. " You will be my witnesses *in Jerusalem* and in all Judea and Samaria, *and* to the end of the earth."[2] This week, we consider both sides of everyday mission. God's command in James, and a theme from Genesis to Revelation, lean toward ordinary people; toward those in need and our neighbors. These are our mission fields, and we cannot ignore either side of those to whom God sends us.

DAY 6

ANSWER
Our workplaces
and schools are
our mission field

READ
1 Corinthians
7:12–26

MISSION IN THE CRACKS

WHERE DO YOU SPEND MOST OF YOUR TIME?

From at least as early as the Greek poet Homer in the eighth century BC, "neighbor" means "people in close, natural proximity to yourself."[3] Today and tomorrow consider the "love your neighbors" side of the everyday mission coin. So again, where do you spend most of your time? Putting aside those heavenly five to nine hours of sleep each night, most of our time each week find us in three places: work, school, and/or home. Today we consider mission at work and school, and tomorrow our homes.

MISSION IS YOUR VOCATION

If you're in your mid-twenties or younger, you likely spend much of any given week involved in some sort of schooling. If older than that, you likely spend as much if not more time at work. We're addressing these together as "mission in our vocation." Consider the similarities. We're either in an occupation or preparing for one. For both school and work, we go somewhere, interact with others, and focus on a common goal. Maybe that goal is a lab experiment or class assignment; maybe it's a sales presentation or *giving* a class their assignment. We're there several hours, and while there we're "on the clock," performing assigned duties and abiding by agreed-upon policies. Work and school have set start and end times, after which we all disperse to our homes and activities.

Few people will argue that one's job is a vocation. In fact, "job" and "vocation" have become so intertwined in today's culture that vocational schools are an alternative to traditional colleges, training students in the skills needed for a specific field. But the original word, "vocation," was not limited to describing one's job or field: the Latin root of the word—actually Christian in origin—describes "a calling." So it's right to label our jobs—or to call the school where we prepare for a job—a "vocation": as we see them as a calling, we find greater meaning and purpose than if they're simply means to cover our mortgage or afford Discovery HD.

EVERY CHRISTIAN IS TRI-VOCATIONAL

"Bivocational" has long been a word that pastors use to describe the fact that some have two jobs: traditionally, one job is "in ministry" and the other is "not." Both Bob and I are bivocational. Typically, it's viewed a negative term, as if bivocational pastors are lower-status than those who work full-time in their church. In fact, many bivocational conferences center on ways to get out of the second job. This low view of bivocationality unintentionally leads others into a poor understanding of the word. In the historical use of the word, every Christian is bi- or tri- or more- vocational.

As early as fifteenth century Christianity, one's vocation referred to one's call by God. God *called* people to Himself. So one's first vocation was salvation. Likewise, one was *called* to the priesthood of all believers—that was a second vocation. And at least as early as medieval Catholicism, specific roles, like marriage and celibacy as well as priesthood and laity, were also labeled vocations—unique callings by God on one's life.[4] If we believe the full historical sense of "vocation," we start to understand God's call to mission at work or school.

Our primary calling is to God; our second calling is to His mission and ministry. This was our theme last week. These two vocations apply to every Christian, regardless of life's situations. But those *general* callings inform our *specific* callings. Our jobs, workplaces, schools, and relationships are some elements of our specific vocations. They're specific arenas given by God in which our general vocations are on display. In Christ, we're each called to God. We're called to mission and ministry. And we're called to a workplace or school to live out that mission and ministry. In that sense, we're each tri-vocational.

PAID MISSIONARIES TO OUR WORK AND SCHOOL

So how does this apply to work and school? Paul speaks to our specific calling in today's passage. While the language might bog us down, consider the overarching theme: using specific examples—the unmarried spouse, the uncircumcised Gentile, and the slave, God shows us that the specific life we have is from Him. Everything we do, everyone we meet, every opportunity we have, is part of a specific vocation, assigned by God. For the Christian, the idea of a specific calling gives meaning and purpose to every meeting, group project, chemistry lab, workshop, and classroom. In our specific vocations, we build relationships. We love, serve, and bless people. We "work heartily, as for the Lord and not for men."[5] We pray for those around us and seek their redemption.

God not only provides our calling; He also supports us in it. Whether paycheck or scholarship, if "every good gift and every perfect gift is from above,"[6] then our friend Jeff Vanderstelt, founder of Soma Communities in Washington, is right: "Whether you get your paycheck with a little stamp that says your church's name, or Microsoft in our case, or Starbucks, or Boeing, or wherever it may be, God is routing His money—His resource—to you through some other company, so that you can be paid for full-time ministry wherever He sends you. [This] means that every single person in [every] church is a full-time, paid minister of the gospel of Jesus Christ."[7]

MISSION "IN THE CRACKS"

Mission at work and school can be tricky. We can't start the day with an office-wide Bible study, spend our morning going from cubicle to cubicle or classroom to classroom, striking up a conversation and making sure we talk about Jesus before we head to the next coworker. After lunch, we don't call everyone to pray before our board meeting. We don't stand up in our freshman biology lecture to proclaim Christ. Whether work or school—whether you're getting paid or are paying to be there—you can, and must live on mission. But mission may likely fit in the "cracks" of your work or school routine: breakfasts, lunches, happy hours, smoke breaks, inviting coworkers over to dinner, or spending time together outside your daily requirements.

Two of my co-elders—both named Matt—often pray on their business trips for God to open doors to conversation with their coworkers and clients. Instead of retiring to their hotel rooms at a decent hour, they've both sat at lobby bars until far too late, as God granted their requests. Brad and Robert are university students who dropped out of Christian campus organizations and church sports leagues, for the sake of living as a missionary to a fraternity, social organization, or campus league. Bob and I both know men and

101 WAYS TO DEMONSTRATE THE GOSPEL

16 Work in a public space: Even if you have the opportunity for a corner office, choose a space you can interact with coworkers. If possible, telecommute from your neighborhood, coffee shop, or pub.

17 Invite the new guy to lunch: Remember how nervous you were on your first day, and bless him with good food and a first office friendship.

18 Spend lunch hours and coffee breaks with coworkers: Instead of retreating for a few moments, eat in the break room or café next door. If that won't work, shoot for happy hour or breakfast.

19 Invite coworkers into nonwork life: After a few meals or drinks, invite them to your home, family, and community. Make individual relationships corporate through meals and hobbies.

women who have rearranged their family budget in order to go to lunch with coworkers instead of dining alone at their desks. We've seen stay-at-home moms form babysitter-swaps with other moms, spending time together, serving each other, and blessing not-yet-believing moms instead of forming Christian-only mommy clusters.

NEGLECTING OUR VOCATIONS?

There are three ways to see this balance of general and specific vocations: one extreme says we ignore the fact that God has a hand in specific jobs or life situations, and claim that our only call is to believe the gospel and live a holy life. In this view, there is only general vocation: work means nothing, or "vocational ministry" is the only work we should pursue. The other extreme ignores the fact that we're called to God and His ministry, and limits vocation to our job or training. In this view, there is only specific vocation: work or school is somehow separate from our "Christian lives." Our faith is limited to Sunday mornings and church events. Instead of either of these, our hope is to land in the biblical middle: to realize God's work, provision, and charge in calling us to Himself and His ministry and in assigning us to the specific elements of our daily life. Our specific vocations fit within our general vocation: work or school is a means by which we live out our general vocation.

Do we consider our nine to five jobs in this light? Do we pray mission opportunities on the first day of every semester? Whatever role we play for forty-plus hours a week, is a specific vocation in which God calls you to live out our general vocation: our gospel identity and His gospel mission.

DID *SESAME STREET* GET IT RIGHT?

DAY 7

WHO ARE THE PEOPLE IN YOUR NEIGHBORHOOD?

With an almost-four- and almost-two-year-old, I'm allowed to quote *Sesame Street* as an authority. In more than thirty episodes of the long-running PBS show, a famous song asks, "Who are the people in your neighborhood?" The song answers the question as furry puppets sing about the postman, laundryman, firefighter, and other local business-puppets, all of whom interact on the 100 block of Sesame Street. As the song closes, it summarizes the answer: "They're the people that you meet, as you're walking down the street; they're the people that you meet each day."[8]

After work or school, you might go to happy hour or the gym. You might meet friends for dinner, take your kids to practice, or run errands. If it's a weekend, we might head out of town. But no matter what you do when you leave the vocation we looked at yesterday, you always, eventually end up in one place: your home. As we said yesterday, "neighbor" has always referred to "people in close, natural proximity to yourself." Unless we work from home, or live on campus or in a commune, God gives us an even closer

ANSWER
Our actual, literal neighbors are our mission field

READ
James 2:8–13

mission field than our vocations. Today we consider the depth of God's command to "love your neighbors."

MISSION IN YOUR 'HOOD

Nine times in the Bible, one command is said to sum up the Old Testament law: "Love your neighbor as yourself."[9] At first glance, "neighbor" in the Bible doesn't seem to connote proximity. In fact, it doesn't seem to have any more specific definition than "those God puts in His people's paths." In fact, if we look at the nine passages, "neighbor" refers to loving . . .

1. other Israelites

2. people you liked (as opposed to "your enemy")

3. other Christians

4. someone who walks into a church gathering for the first time

5. unspecified people in general

6. a nonbeliever who helped a believing stranger in need

While some attempts have been made to broaden "neighbor" to mean "anyone it's convenient for me to love," we must get out of our contemporary, commuter mindsets and back to an ancient, rural world. When we consider the context, we realize that indeed, in all but #6 above (the story of the Good Samaritan), "neighbors" actually were defined by their natural proximity:[10]

1. Israel was one big mobile commune for forty years; everyone lived close to each other.

2. You have to know someone really well to either like them or call them an "enemy".

3. Early churches were small. Many met in homes; they lived in tight-knit community.

4. Someone joining the community for the first time likely wasn't a believer, but since churches didn't have signs,

websites, or buildings, he likely knew someone well enough to be invited.

5. In rural Israel, like much of the world still today, people lived in the same city—if not the same house—their whole lives. So even without specifying whom "neighbor" refers to, hearers likely thought of those in proximity to themselves.

Why does this context matter? Because God sends His people on location-based mission: in fact, as small as Christian communities were, and the fact that many people never moved away from their hometown, that was likely the only kind of mission many early Christians knew. If, as we saw last week in Jeremiah 29, God sends us exactly where He wants us for the sake of His mission, then that mission involves those in close proximity to us. The call is more literal than we often consider it: wherever you live, whoever you are, "love your [actual] neighbors." In fact, in a few places, the Bible even warns us if we do not intentionally pursue love, mercy, grace, and respect to those in our natural proximity.[11]

PRIORITIZING OUR LOCATIONS

Think of the practical implications of neighborhood-based mission—especially in light of the fact that many of us claim that God sovereignly orchestrates every aspect of our lives. We each sleep most nights and eat many meals in our neighborhoods. We keep up with our homes and yards in our neighborhoods. We often relax, take walks, play, and watch TV in our neighborhoods. In many neighborhoods across the world, it's natural to both suffer and celebrate various life events with neighbors. And one of the largest chunks of our monthly budgets—whether renting or especially buying a home—goes toward property in our neighborhoods.

Even more importantly, there's a distinction between mission in our vocation and our locations: while we might spend most of our waking hours at work or school, and while God has indeed sent us on mission there, most of the *free* hours of our week can be spent at home. Neighborhood mission doesn't have to fit in the "cracks" like it does at work or school. Everyday mission can happen freely, as we carry out God's command to love our neighbors.

Both Bob's church and mine are built around neighborhood-based communities. The priority for both of us is mission by location. We'll see this more next week, but every neighborhood provides many potential points of connection with others. You *can* share schools, parks, neighborhood associations, or apartment complexes with those who live near you. You *can* naturally go to the same grocer, gas station, and restaurants as others in your neighborhood, because they're nearby. You have the same city council member, state representative, and even police and fire stations. You *can* see your neighbors more naturally than coworkers or even extended family, because your proximity allows you to interact, borrow flour, attend neighborhood events, and go to school plays and peewee football games together.

IT'S HARD TO LOVE OUR NEIGHBORS

But while all these things *can* happen, it's up to us to decide whether or not they *will*. It may look different than vocational mission, but loving neighbors takes just as much intentionality and sacrifice as loving coworkers and classmates. Simply living in a mission field isn't enough; we must live there as a missionary. So we might invite neighbors over for dinner instead of going out. We might rearrange our schedules to be home when they are. We might do more things in our neighborhoods than we used to. And we have to be proactive: we have to actually meet our neighbors—even if we might offend them; even if they're weird or think we are.

The gospel is divisive. As the saying goes, "Never talk about religion or politics." In many situations, relationships change when faith enters a conversation. It's even more difficult if we've lived near or worked with someone for many years. The last Sunday of every month, The City Church scatters: we worship God by obeying biblical commands that Christians aren't known for obeying well. "Love Your Neighbor Sundays" see our church family throwing block parties, inviting others over, pulling out grills, baking cookies for hermits, and so forth. One couple had lived next to their neighbors for a decade when their first time a Love Your Neighbors Sunday came around. They were embarrassed that the extent of their relationship was a "what's-up?" nod exchanged between the men as they got in their cars every morning. They worked through their fears and shame, and their first act of loving their neighbors was ringing the bell armed with cookies and wine. And repenting. "We've lived next to you for years, but don't even know you. We'd like to be better neighbors; will you give us a chance?" That first step was hard. But the neighbors responded well, and now they have regular interaction, and even talk about faith.

This isn't just true in a city. Bob lives on mission in the suburbs, and I grew up on a fourteen-acre farm. My family grew hay, and I paid for part of college from showing sheep and goats, who were loaded onto a trailer once sold, "to go their new home" we were told (may they rest in peace). At least three football fields could have been built between our front door and our neighbors', so mission had to look different than it does in apartment buildings or city blocks. But it could still happen. Communities rallied around sports, livestock, and rodeo events, and came together for harvest. We helped each

101 WAYS TO DEMONSTRATE THE GOSPEL

20 Build short fences: Tall fences don't actually make good neighbors; they distance and privatize you. Remove fences between you and your neighbors, or if you must have them, build them low.

21 Serve your neighbors: Help with yard work, then enjoy a tasty beverage and admire your shared masterpiece. Pick up mail when they leave town. Babysit on their date night. Get creative.

22 Host events: Summer barbecues, movie nights on your lawn, a community garden, progressive dinners—all offer opportunities for neighbors to involve themselves in one another's lives.

other with the never-ending care of crops, and worked together to protect our animals from coyotes. We held bonfires and hayrides. Kids hiked the fields together. Mission looks different in cities, suburbs, and farms. But with creative commitment, it can still happen.

Who are the people in your neighborhood? Yes, they can be the people that you meet each day—but it takes intentionality, and it takes realizing they're the people to whom God sent you, on His difficult but vital mission. Who knew Jim Henson's kid show was so biblical?[12]

UNLIKELY BROTHERS

"WE'RE SOME OF THE BEST-FED PEOPLE IN FORT WORTH."

I wasn't in a country club when I heard these words, nor a steakhouse, or even a wedding reception. A guy I'll call Rodney told me this, sitting on the curb outside the homeless shelter where he was staying on East Lancaster. Fort Worth's homeless row was recently named the #15 Most Dangerous Neighborhood in the U.S.[13] Some friends had been there for a few hours, playing football, Frisbee, and guitars, talking and laughing with the folks whose only "home" kicks them out every day to sanitize and prepare for that night's influx of tenants. Rodney and I had been talking about education and sports, but were interrupted by a pickup truck's arrival. A couple guys jumped out of the truck and started unloading Styrofoam boxes of food to the gathering crowd.

"You gonna go eat?" I asked. "Nah," Rodney replied, "I'm still full from the otha' truck. And watch: most of them aren't gonna eat either." I hadn't seen this otha' truck, but sure enough, I watched as many of the gathered diners grabbed Styrofoam boxes, looked to see what was in them, and walked away empty-handed. "Explain this to me," I said. "Man, we're some of the best-fed people in Fort Worth. Everyday people

ANSWER
The marginalized in our society are our mission field

READ
Matthew
25:31–46

come here, givin' us leftovers and feelin' good 'bout themselves. This is the third or fourth truck today. But you know what? They don't care 'bout me. They don't wanna know my name. They wanna give us stuff and get away from here; go back home and forget us."

As someone who had brought food before and led groups of teenagers to serve food to homeless shelters, I was admittedly stunned. "Well, if you don't need food, what is it you need?" Rodney looked into my eyes for one of the only times in our entire conversation. He said in a flash of sad anger, "Man, we want the same as everyone else want, man! We wanna be loved. We wanna know people. And we want people to know us." I stared back in silence. In an instant, I realized that my view of "serving the poor" was a massive failure.

THE PLACE OF SERVICE IN MISSION

As we look at this side of everyday mission, we can't help but consider Matthew 25. Jesus' words about clothing and feeding those in need are dismissed by evangelicals at times, because they've been tied to the "social gospel movement." We're not proponents of that movement, where "the gospel" primarily (or exclusively) deals with meeting physical needs. But the gospel is social. Standing before God one day, this text teaches us that all of us will answer for our service. To ignore a principle because someone abused or mistranslated it is as dangerous as those who abuse and mistranslate in the first place. On one hand, even Jesus' own kingdom proclamation was surrounded by healings, miracles, and other blessings. We cannot ignore the place of "good works, which God prepared beforehand that we should walk in them,"[14] in our gospel call. On the other hand, as Kevin DeYoung and Greg Gilbert have pointed out, "The minute you start arguing that good works are not of *the utmost importance*, people accuse you of saying they are of no importance at all."[15] These authors summarize biblical motives for gospel service: "We do good works to obey God, whom we love, . . . because we love our neighbors, . . . to show the world God's character and God's work, . . . because they are the fruit of the Spirit's work in us, [and] . . . to win a hearing for the gospel."[16]

I (Bob) didn't believe it when I heard about one Vietnamese man coming to faith in Christ. I knew him well and figured someone must have misunderstood. I was with him a few weeks later and I asked him where he was with Jesus. He told me, "I accepted Him." I was excited, and I wondered what had changed him. "I saw doctors coming to serving the sick, plumbers coming to purify our water, teachers coming to teach our kids. When my dad died, I began to think about the meaning of life and concluded that there had to be God. The best example I saw of Him was in those people." Versions of that same story have been told over and over again, by different people in the housing projects our members work in and other projects.

Echoing God's charge that Abraham be a blessing,[17] we tell people often that we serve not to convert—we serve because we've been converted. This is a vital distinction, but service and proclamation go hand in hand. We must *proclaim* a message, but those around us need to see that message in action. Proclamation is most powerful in the context of a loving, caring, serving relationship. As I (Bob) write this, I'm preparing to take Vietnamese diplomats to meet some of our nation's leaders in Washington, DC. One Vietnamese ambassador once introduced me to other ambassadors as the "American Ambassador to Vietnam in America." These relationships exist only because of NorthWood's members and how they devoted themselves to Vietnam for over twenty years. Jesus healed, fed, and delivered. He showed people gospel-driven service, as we do those things too. That's a picture of loving the "least of these." We serve in the name of Jesus.

HOW CAN THIS LOOK IN AN EVERYDAY SETTING?

Back in the U.S., some in The City Church family started a local organization called The NET. On one hand, it's a "safety net" for those in homelessness, low-income neighborhoods, and sexual exploitation; on the other hand it "networks" churches, nonprofits, and individuals, seeking "to empower the city to restore dignity to those in poverty through community and relationships."[18] Having

seen disproportionate favor in our city, from the homeless community to even the local government, Melissa, Jimmy, Sarah, and
their team train people how to not only do nice things for those in
need, but also to build relationships with them. Through their work,
The NET has seen many from their "street family" get jobs. They've
seen prostitutes, in and out of jail for decades, work through The
NET's rehab and discipleship program and be truly loved for the
first time. But more importantly, they've seen some of the most
difficult people in our city discuss faith for the first time ever. And
most importantly, they've seen God draw people to Himself.

One way The City Church scatters to worship is serving our city.
Every Serve Sunday, multiple areas of need in our city look like an
HGTV show: trucks pull up full of supplies and dozens of people
converge on each area. We build, clean, repair, paint, and practically serve. But as much as we can help it, these projects are never
one-time, disconnected events. At some point, we gather everyone
together, talk about each organization, and ask our church family
how they can be involved in long-term ways, creating ongoing opportunity to demonstrate the gospel.

What started as painting a low-income school and building a
playground has turned into regular tutoring, hosting education-
based Halloween and Christmas events for students who shouldn't
go out after dark and might not get presents, and blessing school
staff throughout the year. What started as repairing a transition
home for prostitutes has evolved into a team of ladies who disciple
prostitutes out of the sex industry. What started as a big event for
Fort Worth's street family turned into a homeless man staying on
a family's couch, and later breaking his tough façade enough to tell
the husband through tears, "No one has ever loved me like this."

IT'S HARD TO LOVE THOSE IN NEED

Loving those in need is difficult because it asks us to go out of
our way. Unless we work in certain jobs, it's unlikely that we spend
regular, quality time with an orphan, tutoring underprivileged kids,
playing games at a nursing home, or visiting hospitals or prisons.

Too often we consider the first half of Jesus' label—"the least of these my brothers"—while missing the second half. To many of us, widows, orphans, prisoners, the elderly, the sick, the homeless, prostitutes, and refugees, are "the least." They may be low-income, less-clean, and lost in many senses of the word. But while Jesus acknowledges their need, He also calls them "my brothers." There's inherent worth in their neediness; they are created in God's image. Their physical condition reflects the spiritual condition of every human: we need salvation.

You might not start an organization. But there's someone in need near you, and somewhere in your city live marginalized people. Loving them means finding ways to bless them and to build ongoing relationships. We meet needs, build trust, and in a sense "earn the right" to speak into the lives of those in need. It takes sacrifice, relationship, prayer, and time to build trust and get to know people. And the goal of service is to point those in need to their greatest need, who is Jesus.

101 WAYS TO DEMONSTRATE THE GOSPEL

23 Volunteer at a school near you: Nearly every school has more needs than they can fill. Serve however teachers and administration need. Tutor students, and even bless their families at times.

24 Serve with an organization: Don't reinvent the wheel; find groups meeting a need you're passionate about, or become passionate about some local need. Find a group and serve well.

25 Work with organizations that aren't specifically Christian: Bring Christian influence to secular groups. Bless those the organization is serving, but also meet and serve alongside not-yet-believers.

DAY 9

ANSWER
The world—both here and there—is our mission field

READ
Acts 11:19–26

196 NATIONS

"WHAT HAVE WE DONE?"

My (Bob's) wife and I had planned on becoming paid, full-time missionaries, but there were obstacles and that door was never opened. At least not in the way we expected. As I mentioned in this book's intro, seven years into NorthWood's existence, God placed a question in my mind, *What if the church was a missionary?* I thought, "The Great Commission was given to the whole church, and everyone in it—but we've turned it into a job for just a handful of people, and have ignored the rest beyond praying and giving money."

We cannot see everyday mission and global mission as separate from each other. At the very least, followers of Jesus should be the most globally aware people on the face of the earth. For readers who will go to other nations, everyday mission is a training ground now for your global mission one day. For others who will never set foot outside the United States, let's open our eyes to God's work around the world, and *at least* support it through prayer and finance. And whether or not we ever go to other nations, many nations have already come to many of us.

A BIGGER COMMISSION THAN WE KNEW

The Great Commission was not the beginning of God's global mission. It was in Genesis that God gave man dominion over the *whole earth*, and later renamed Abram as Abraham—"the Father of *Nations*." From Israel's priesthood to the nations, to Psalms in praise of His name being exalted among the nations, to many prophets, the proclamation of God's glory and His love for the whole earth is seen throughout the Old Testament, thousands of years before Jesus.

Then all four gospel writers include the Great Commission, each with a nuanced view. Matthew emphasizes our authority to make disciples in all nations. Mark speaks of proclaiming the gospel to all creation in the entire world. Luke focuses on repentance and forgiveness for all nations—this is how we enter the kingdom. John emphasizes our being sent to the world. And in Acts 1, Luke shifts his focus from the physical body of Christ, Jesus, to the spiritual body of Christ, the Church.[19]

The first church started outside Jerusalem was in Antioch. Seen in Acts 11, it was not founded by preachers, but businessmen who moved there for mission. Since much of Acts speaks of Paul and his companions, we might assume that his journeys were the only way global mission happened—but they weren't. The gospel spread to Antioch without any apostle; it went by the hands of ordinary Christians, living on mission. The apostles later sent Barnabas to check it out, and they found its work real and powerful. Then Barnabas sent for Paul to bolster the Antioch mission. The two left but returned in Acts 13. Only then did this church send Paul and Barnabas to Asia Minor. Paul's first missionary journey started from a church planted by everyday Christians—who, in fact, had gone to Antioch to flee persecution by the very man they later commissioned.[20]

GLOBAL MISSION TODAY

There is only one conclusion from the pattern established throughout the Bible: being an everyday disciple on everyday mission is a global enterprise. But what does that look like today? Especially since the early 1800s, global missions have largely become something that vocational preachers or full-time missionaries do. In many churches, global mission is completely removed from local missions. But God's picture and plan of mission is far bigger, more comprehensive, and even inclusive than that. Instead of division, we should see synergy. To that end, we want to encourage four ways everyday missionaries can be involved in God's global mission.

1. Be on Global Mission Without Ever Leaving Your City

Bob and I live in an area where 44 percent of the population—almost half!—was born in non-English speaking nations.[21] The world has come to Dallas–Fort Worth, and the same is true of many US cities. Learning a language, realizing that some of yesterday's marginalized people are from other nations, and serving refugees and asylum seekers are great ways to be involved in those from around the world. Ashley and Kurtis invited two Rwandan asylum seekers into their home once they realized they had nowhere to live. Asylum seekers are internationals who have fled to the United States due to persecution, but who have yet to be granted "protected" status—so they can't get papers to work or legally earn money to live. Word spread, and other asylum seekers arrived at their doorstep. They invited friends into this simple ministry and started raising funds and people to help with living costs. In just two years, DASH Network (DFW-Area Asylum Seeker Housing) has served over thirty asylum seekers. A family in The City Church even bought a small apartment building for DASH housing, which people in our church renovated and help manage.[22] The rest of this book's principles can affect the world right where we are. Then these people can engage others back home—whether returning or through contact from the United States—far better than you or I ever could.

2. Go, Dig In, and Stay

Instead of choosing a different mission trip location every year, or scattering teams to multiple places across the world, what if we prayerfully chose one or two places, and sent our time, skills, and finances there as often as possible? NorthWood adopted Hanoi, Vietnam, and Puebla, Mexico. The City Church is setting up long-term engagement in Ethiopia and another highly Muslim nation. We pursue God's work through orphan prevention and reunification, church planting, and sending people to live in, work, and serve those nations through their professions and passions. Our desire is to make a deep, focused impact, instead of a shallow, wide one.

3. Use Your Job, Skills, and Passion

In the past, global missionaries' focus was preaching or doing religious work. In more and more places, this is becoming impossible. And many nations are seeing through our thin façade of "teaching English." But what if we saw our jobs as a skill the rest of the world needs? Vicky is an executive at Fidelity who has mentored emerging businesswomen in Vietnam and done microfinance. James is a professional landscaper who has built corrals for water buffaloes for farmers who are trying to grow their livelihood. Chad is a schoolteacher who teaches physical education in public schools in another nation. If every missionary had to be a pastor and preacher, we'd never have enough to reach the world. Neither will most of us feel qualified. Nor will they be allowed into many places. But just as mission happens in our vocations here, so can it happen there.

4. Build Relationships

We live in a world that is connected like never before. My (Bob's) son runs his businesses in Vietnam from the United States. What if we became students of a particular city in the world over the Internet and social media, began to connect with people there, and found opportunities to do with those people the same things we do for our next-door neighbors? And as you can imagine, two decades of regular work in

Vietnam have led to many strong relationships. Many of my (Bob's) church members are Facebook friends with people all over Vietnam, and are always communicating. Last week there was a serious mudslide in a village in North Vietnam and seven teachers we had trained in an education conference were killed. As we grieved with them from afar, the tragedy has opened up the door for significant ministry.

DESIRE AND EXPOSURE

How can we apply the principles of everyday mission to God's global mission? God always provides for what He calls us to do. People who don't or can't travel do much of NorthWood's global work. We've hosted education conferences in Vietnam for seven years, which require only six to ten travelers, but which require twenty to thirty people stateside to gather the materials and organize. You may not be able to go somewhere globally but once every two or three years. But go when you can. Yes, pray and give—but also go. Somewhere. Once there, learn, serve, develop relationships, share,

101 WAYS
TO DEMONSTRATE THE GOSPEL

26 Serve refugees, asylum seekers, and immigrants: Agencies help you meet them. Show them the city, teach cultural nuances, help them learn English, invite them to meals and holidays.

27 As a community, adopt a people group: Child sponsorship, sending resources, short-term trips, meeting actual and felt needs, and building relationships are all first global steps.

28 Pursue your sister city: Many cities in the United States have a "sister city" in a different country. Learn where your city's is and get involved. In this, you bless your own city and theirs.

29 Build a relationship across the world: Whether through your job or school, a "friend of a friend," or social media connection, pursue people in a nation where God might be leading you to engage.

receive, and build trust. Take opportunities to expose your Western mind to a global need. Serve those who are there long-term. As you do, you have no choice but to fall in love with people.

Following Acts 1:8, we may start in "Jerusalem," but we can't stop there. "Jerusalem and in all Judea and Samaria, and to the end of the earth" describe real, geographic places where God sends people. And from Jerusalem to Antioch to Rome, then eventually to the Western Hemisphere and even to your own life, you're likely a Christian because a string of people chose to obey God's global mandate. As an everyday missionary, find ways to pursue these principles both here and abroad. By all means, carry out God's mission where you live. But don't ignore the rest of the world.

DAY 10

OUR CLOSEST, FORGOTTEN MISSION

THE LARGEST TARGET OF NOT-YET-BELIEVERS WE MAY EVER INTERACT WITH LIVES UNDER OUR OWN ROOFS.

ANSWER
Our families are our mission field

READ
Deuteronomy
6:4–6; 1 Peter
2:25–3:7

As I often tell The City Church parents, there's no one with whom our lives are more shared—no closer "neighbors," if you will—than spouses, kids, parents, and siblings. Everyday mission must not neglect our actual, immediate and extended, family. The City Church has a 2:1 ratio of adults to kids. Some City Groups are at 2:1 . . . kids to adults! We see believers occasionally get a not-yet-believing spouse to join them on a Sunday morning. But it's often easier to get them into someone's home for a cookout or movie night. We know parents who grieve their children's souls. And we know children—college-aged and middle-aged—who beg God for their parents' and siblings' salvation.

GOD'S CALL TO THE FAMILY

Throughout the Bible, God turns His people toward the home. After giving the Shema in Deuteronomy 6, God commands Old Testament Israel to teach this crucial declaration to their children in as many everyday ways as possible. This sentiment is echoed throughout the Old Testament, as God instructs His people to make His ways known to their "children and your children's children."[23] Later, Jesus famously invited children to Himself, even as His disciples pushed them away. And He often used elements of children's faith as a metaphor for the kingdom of God. Some of Jesus' own family members were among His first followers: two of his brothers penned biblical letters, and His brother James was leader at the world's first church.[24]

Family imagery fills the most common metaphors for the Church in the New Testament.[25] Patriarchs and matriarchs of a family are baptized "with their [household] as well."[26] Still true in much of the world today, extended families in Bible times all lived in one home. When a child got married, a room was added to the house and life went on. Children apprenticed to continue the family business. Fathers led families as patriarch pastors. Missional leader Mike Breen (not the sportscaster; this one has an awesome British accent) explains that the Greco-Roman *oikos* ("extended family"—a group of twenty to sevently people) was a primary venue for the gospel spread in the early church.[27] He argues that since families were close-knit, if one person began following Jesus, family members often followed—thus the "household" references in Acts.

We don't live in homes of twenty people today. At most, parents or in-laws may live with us, or a sibling for a season. We might follow Chevy Chase's example of a full house for the holidays, but everyone goes home.[28] We may not live in the same city, or even nation, as our parents. The most often we might see anyone outside our immediate family is at a reunion. In that context, they might be as excited to talk about Jesus as they are about the commemorative iron-on T-shirt your aunt insists on making everyone. But unless your family is uniquely blessed, there are likely people in our own genealogies who don't follow Jesus; some probably reject Him outright. How do we live on mission to our family? We want to suggest two ways, depending on the relationship.

DILIGENTLY TEACH CHILDREN

Parents, the Bible is clear when it comes to your role in your child's life: you are their primary discipler. We cannot farm out our child's spiritual growth to a church, school, camp, or trip. Yes, our community should come alongside us in raising children. And yes, elders must equip us to train our children. But that's another book. *We* are responsible to teach and model the gospel to our kid. Again remembering Deuteronomy 6, we demonstrate the good news to our children, in everyday ways, using everyday objects and stories. We patiently help them grasp the motives behind disobedience. We pray for them, with them, and have them pray even if they don't "get it." We explain baptism and communion while they watch us partake of it. We read the Bible, lead family worship, and ensure intentional times of prayer. I love the fact that even though she has no idea what she's really doing, as early as eighteen-months-old, Maggie clasps her hands, squints her eyes, and bows her curls to pray, and joins in with an "ah-mehh" at the end. In these and much more, God sends us on mission to those He's most-closely entrusted to us. Our babies are part of our mission field.

I (Bob) took my son to Vietnam for the first time when he was ten. He is now a businessman who wants to do business for God's glory, and has been many times since. So he started a few small businesses there. In addition his work with global education, one of his businesses is selling portraits. Some Vietnamese artists can paint a perfect replica of any photograph you give them, for far less than the hundreds—or thousands—of dollars paintings can cost in the United States. For only $200 you can have a beautiful family portrait. Most of his income comes from the education job, but portraits have become roads to relationships with many young painters. He once told me, "I didn't feel like I was doing that much good until I realized this has provided income for ten families for several months. That really changed my perception." I am a proud dad.

BE FAITHFUL TO ADULTS

If "diligence" is the key exhortation toward mission to children, "faithfulness" might be the key word for mission to not-yet-believing adults in our families. It echoes the "honor" commanded toward parents on God's Sinai stones in Exodus. And it follows 1 Peter 3's exhortation to wives' attitudes toward unbelieving husbands.[29] In today's verse, Jesus' own example of a shepherd laying down his life for lost sheep is the basis for Peter's encouragement, to servants toward their masters, wives toward unbelieving husbands, husbands toward presumably unbelieving wives, and every Christian toward every authority. As Jesus patiently laid down His own life for us, so we are sent to the unbelieving adults in our families. As Jesus revealed the character and work of God in His words, actions, death, and resurrection, so we can reveal the character and work of God in our words, actions, and death to self. We are faithful to those sheep in our own flock who have wandered away.

In many ways, mission to young children resembles mission to those in need: though we're in their lives every day, we have to be creative and intentional, meet their needs, and lay down our lives to teach them and discuss faith on a level that isn't common to adult conversation. Whatever the age of our children, sacrificing for the sake of leading our children is right and good: by God's grace, we reflect Him as we meet our kids' needs, both physically and spiritually. And in many ways, mission to our adult families resembles the ways we engage our neighbors: while we may have to go out of our way to see them if they live far away, we can have deep relationships; we can spend time and know pain and joys; we have history and know points of gospel connection.

OUR #1 PRIORITY?

We must close today with an important question: Is family a *more primary mission field than nonfamily?* We're certain that many would answer "yes" without a moment's hesitation. But while Jesus' own family became believers He did not seem to allow His heartstrings to be tugged exclusively to His parents and siblings. "Whoever loves father or mother more than me is not worthy of me, and whoever loves son or daughter more than me is not worthy of me," while "Everyone who has left houses or brothers or sisters or father or mother or children or lands, for my name's sake, will receive a hundredfold and will inherit eternal life."[30] Before they believed He was the Messiah, Jesus' family rejected Him. But that did not deter Him from his mission to fishermen, tax collectors, and prostitutes. At one point when His family sought to speak to—and likely distract— Him, His response seems downright harsh: "'Who is my mother, and who are my brothers?' . . . He said, 'Here are my mother and my brothers! For whoever does the will of my Father in heaven is my brother and sister and mother.'"[31]

This week's push is for mission wherever God has sent us. So on one hand, our family is the closest, most heartfelt mission field. On the other hand, we must guard against "family idolatry"—putting more value on our families, simply because we have longer history and an abiding love for them than our neighbors and coworkers. So is mission to family *primary*? It must not be lost as a priority, but the

101 WAYS TO DEMONSTRATE THE GOSPEL

30 Start when they're young: The earlier your child hears you pray, talk about the gospel, model fruit of the Spirit, etc, the better. Intentionally train your child, before you think you should.

31 Be proactive with extended family: If they live nearby, initiate get-togethers and include them in celebrations. If farther away, call or video chat. Check up; let them know you're praying for them.

32 Bless your family: Be the first to meet needs. Be the most generous with giving gifts or providing food. Be the first to both repent and forgive. And be willing to explain why.

safest biblical line to draw is that we must guard our emotions, motives, and idols from making it *the* priority. We must neither ignore our families for the sake of everyday mission, nor ignore everyday mission for the exclusive sake of our families.

"WHO" QUESTIONS FOR YOU TO WORK THROUGH

☐ **GENERAL**: What impacted you the most this week? What was new, convicting, or confusing? What was difficult? What do you need to discuss with others?

☐ **GENERAL**: Where's your heart, as you consider God's mission? What are you currently thinking? What's motivating you? What scares you? How is God moving in you?

☐ **DAY 6**: List the people you interact with regularly in your vocation. Who among them are followers of Jesus? Who aren't? Who aren't you sure about? (If you don't interact with people at work or school, why not?)

☐ **DAY 6**: What are some of the "cracks" of your normal workweek during which you could spend time with your coworkers? What would it take for you to do so?

☐ **DAY 7**: List the people you interact with regularly in your neighborhood. Who among them are followers of Jesus? Who aren't? Who aren't you sure about? (If you don't interact with people in your neighborhood, why not?)

☐ **DAY 7**: What are some of the times and rhythms of your week that you could spend time with neighbors? What would it take for you to do so?

☐ **DAY 8**: What has been your experience with those in need? How do you see pursuing them as reflecting the character and work of God seen in the gospel?

☐ **DAY 8:** In what specific ways might you build a bridge into serving the marginalized in your city, and build meaningful relationships?

☐ **DAY 9:** What has been your view of global missions? What has been your involvement?

DAY 9: How can you become more involved in God's global mandate, through opportunities both locally and abroad?

☐ **DAY 10:** If you have kids, how have you seen them as a mission field? What are ways you can "diligently teach them"—by words, actions, and everyday moments—the words and ways of God?

☐ **DAY 10:** What adults in your family are not yet believers? What would "faithfulness" look like for you to display and declare the gospel to each of them? What are some attributes of God that would be particularly meaningful for each to realize?

☐ **GENERAL:** Look back over this week's "Everyday Mission Ideas." What additional, practical things can you come up with, specific to your personality, gifting, and mission field, to live out God's mission? Share your ideas online with the hashtag #everydaymission.

MY MISSION
RICK MCKINLEY

PORTLAND, OREGON

In the early days of Imago Dei Community we desired to show the city that Jesus loved Portland. We started a bottom-up approach where people found places of need and rallied the congregation to join in. I guess you could call it a movement. We called it "Love Portland." The first year was a great success: we redeemed an abandoned park that had

been taken over with used needles, overgrown bushes, and the dream of a thousand children that would never "darken the door" of this park, because no parent would currently allow their kids to play there.

In twenty-four hours the place was transformed, and the neighborhood noticed. For the first time in years children played in that park and felt safe. As time progressed we continued to Love Portland, creating new ways in

which we could love our city. But we noticed something: as a whole, the city didn't really feel the love. Sure, there were people who did, but overall the 1.9 million people of Portland didn't even know we existed, let alone see us love them in Jesus' name.

Then it hit us: "What if we asked the leaders of our city what the biggest needs were, and made those our needs too?" We started to call the mayor and ask for a meeting. Now Portland is a proudly progressive city, and any mayor who would take a church's call would have been putting himself or herself at risk. But we kept calling. And the mayors came and went without answering. But after one new mayor took office, the unexpected happened.

Sam Adams was both the first openly gay mayor in a city of our size, and the first mayor to answer our call. In the years that we had been calling to find out what the city needed, we also began collaborating with Luis Palau Association. Luis is one of my heroes, and Kevin Palau, the president of LPA, became a close friend. We began to dream together what it would look like to rally thousands of Christians to serve the city. When we met with Mayor Adams and asked what the biggest needs of the city were, he told us three things: the high school dropout rate, the condition of school facilities, and the sex trafficking epidemic in Portland. Since these were what the city was facing, we committed to join in and make the city's issues our issues. We are not people living outside the city; we are part of the city and are here to display the kingdom of Jesus where we live.

The partnership went amazingly well. Sam took a lot of heat from the LGBTQ community for partnering with evangelicals. Surprisingly, we didn't take nearly as much heat as we thought we would. In fact many local churches joined in, to the point that over twenty thousand people volunteered to work at public schools. The movement has grown from that day into a sustainable mission with hundreds of churches truly loving Portland. We have partnered with the city in areas of sex trafficking advocacy, public school partnerships, medical and dental care, helping the home-

less, and caring for the environment. Sam Adams called it the greatest volunteer effort in the history of Portland.

Today we have a new mayor and are enjoying a good relationship with him. But we also have relationships throughout the city government and are respected in the city. The superintendent of Portland public schools has asked that every school partner with a church. Seventy-plus churches have rallied to care for the children in the foster system and support families that are fostering children, while working to help those who have lost their children create a safe home so that their children can come home.

There are so many stories I could tell, but the point is not how great the church has been. The truth is that we are not a faithful people, but we are a redeemed people who are joining Jesus as He loves our city. Thus we get to participate in everyday miracles as Jesus and His kingdom break into our city with hope, redemption, and salvation. We feel grateful that we get to be a part of that. And what's more, the city is feeling the love.

RICK MCKINLEY serves as lead pastor of Imago Dei Community. He is the cocreator of Love Portland and Advent Conspiracy, a global initiative designed to help solve the water crisis by calling Christians back to the real meaning of Christmas. Rick is also an author, professor, and speaker. rickmckinley.net

WHAT DOES AN EVERYDAY MISSIONARY DO?

Jesus, the Bible, the Church, and the clergy each held a prominent place in Western society from as early as the fourth century AD, an era now called "Christendom." But "held" is a past-tense word. British leader Stuart Murray, among many other experts, claims that Western society has largely shifted from Christendom to post-Christendom, which is "the culture that emerges as the Christian faith loses coherence within a society that has been definitively shaped by the Christian story, and as institutions that have been developed to express Christian convictions decline in influence."* Murray gives seven transitions that mark that shift:

1. "From center to margins: In Christendom, the Christian story and churches were central, but in post-Christendom these are marginal.

2. From majority to minority: In Christendom Christians comprised the (often overwhelming) majority, but in post-Christendom we are a minority.

3. From settlers to sojourners: In Christendom Christians felt at home in a culture shaped by [our] story, but in post-Christendom we are aliens, exiles, and pilgrims in a culture where we no longer feel at home.

4. From privilege to plurality: In Christendom Christians enjoyed many privileges, but in post-Christendom, we are one community among many in a pluralistic society.

5. From control to witness: In Christendom Christian churches could exert control over society, but in post-Christendom we exercise influence only through witnessing to our story and its implications.

6. From maintenance to mission: In Christendom the emphasis was on maintaining the supposedly Christian status quo, but in post-Christendom, it must be on mission within a contested environment.

7. From institution to movement: In Christendom churches operated mainly in an institutional mode, but in post-Christendom, we must again become a movement."

How many of those transitions have happened, or are happening, in your mission field? Or at least, what glimpses do you see of the impending change? This shift leads to this week's question: "WHAT does an everyday missionary do?" Murray boils the answer down to two options: we either bury our heads in the sand and continue as if society isn't changing, or we embrace the new reality and reshape our mission. As you might guess, this week we provide ways to equip you for the latter.

---

* This quote and 1–7 list below from Stuart Murray, *Post-Christendom: Church and Mission in a Strange New World* (Carlisle PA: Paternoster, 2004), 11–12.

THE VIEW FROM 30,000 FEET

FORT WORTH IS A BEAUTIFUL, MESSED-UP CITY, AND WE BOTH LOVE IT.

I live near downtown; Bob's just outside Fort Worth's north Loop. At the time of this writing, "Cowtown" is the second-fastest-growing large city in the United States. We'll be over one million strong by 2030, with twenty thousand new living units being built in three miles of downtown. They're largely apartments, condos, and lofts on top of trendy ground floor retail and restaurants. We have great bike trails that you have to share with horses. We're even rerouting the Trinity River to include a lake and water park. Wanna come live on mission with us? Patterned after downtown Portland, Oregon, Fort Worth is becoming a hot place. (Literally: it'll definitely be warmer here than Portland.)

In the midst of the progress, 75 percent of our city is unchurched. That's high for the traditional middle of the Bible Belt. As of a few years ago, twenty thousand refugees live here from forty-five ethnic groups. Eight thousand people need nursing care but can't afford it. Between four and five thousand homeless roam our streets, over 60 percent of whom are women and children. One out of every six males and one out of every

ANSWER
Everyday missionaries see the big picture

READ
Acts 17:16–31

four females is sexually abused before age eighteen. We're home to two to three hundred gangs, with five to six thousand members. We're not comparing our city to yours; we're simply stating facts.[1] This is the broken city we love. Really, wanna come live on mission with us?

How well do you know your own culture? Whether city, town, suburb, community, farm, neighborhood, nudist hippie commune, or wherever you call the place you live, how well do you know the neighbors and those in need we introduced last week? A missionary gets to know the mission field they've been sent to. Tomorrow we look at the personal side of getting to know it, but today we look at—to borrow a cross-cultural mission term—the whole "people group."

YOUR MISSION FIELD'S STATISTICS

The first approach to learning our city is to see the big picture. All the statistics above were pulled from publicly available resources. We can each find at least some information about our mission fields through online and print media. Here are a few pockets of missionary gold:

→ City websites: find your city's official site, but also look at visitors' bureaus, chambers of commerce, schools, and local businesses or organizations.

→ Organization and unofficial sites: for example, look up your city's museums, arts and cultural websites, opinion sites, food and drink blogs, and community events.

→ Newspapers and television/radio stations: again, spend time with the sources of official news, but also look for neighborhood newsletters or Internet sites, cultural magazines, etc.

→ Look up your city on Wikipedia or in state almanacs, government publications, and so on.

All of these help paint a picture of the places God has sent us. We learn demographics, socioeconomics, areas of growth, and needs.

We see the public presentation and perception of our cultures, and will likely be astounded by cultural divisions of our cities.

YOUR MISSION FIELD'S STORIES

Everyone has stories. Some are personal; many are shared with others. One person might be traumatized by an auto accident, but an entire community might mourn the loss of a beloved neighbor. A raise might impact a family, while excitement at their baby's birth ripples through their extended community. Each of our mission fields are filled with stories, some personal and some corporate. Everyday missionaries learn the stories of our mission fields for two reasons. First, stories help display worldviews, values, and beliefs. Second, stories show points of rejection or connection to the gospel. What do we listen for as we hear stories? Here are a few elements:

→ What's this person's/community's history?

→ Where do they find their identity? In what do they put their hope?

→ What are "wins and losses" this person/community has faced?

→ What wounds exist? What are they hardened to?

→ What do they love? What do they spend time and money on?

→ What does this person/community value?

→ In what ways are they indignant; in what areas do they feel entitled?

→ What false gods or idols exist in their personal/corporate life?

Fort Worth began as a tiny military outpost, which became a vital stop on cattle trails. Then we became a major source of railroad shipping, after local citizens' own funds and hands built rails when the tracks lost funding just west of rival Dallas. We then became home to some progressive financial institutions, then colleges, and are still touted by our city's official website as being "the most Texan of all Texas cities."[2] Our city's history is one of pulling ourselves up by literal bootstraps, of pitching in for the good of the city, and of general wealth. Though some of these events happened 150-plus years ago, their influence still echoes, oddly reminiscent of generational blessing and generational sin in the Old Testament. Fort Worth is still ruggedly individualistic, even in its urbanism. The "macho cowboy" mentality still largely reigns, even for those who hung up their boots generations ago. Citizens—especially those who have lived here long—deeply value the general "welfare of the city." While we are economically diverse, it's hard to find an area without idols of comfort and wealth: folks either have it or want it. And we still hate Dallas (at least in jest). If we pay attention, we can apply the gospel to those passions, idols, values, and needs.

PAUL AND THE CULTURE OF ATHENS

City stats and stories help us learn two elements of our mission fields. Demographics, socioeconomic studies, and neighborhood analyses can point out the neediest parts of our communities. And getting to know the natural rhythms of those closest to us helps us engage our neighbors in meaningful moments and ways. We want to close today with one biblical model of learning a city's culture for

101 WAYS
TO DEMONSTRATE THE GOSPEL

33 Know the things that shape culture: Watch movies and TV shows, listen to music, read books. At least find reviews of the major ones and know enough to see points of brokenness and engagement.

34 Visit public places one Sunday morning: Go to a park, running trail, coffeeshop, or store. Don't do this every week, but see once what the rest of the world does while you're in a church gathering.

35 Hang out in your 'hood on a Sunday morning: do the same thing as #34, but do it at home. See who's out, watch interactions, talk to folks, even make brunch and invite them over.

the sake of mission. Reread today's passage from Acts 17. It's long, but worth a careful read. As you read, circle (or highlight, you e-readers) elements of Athenian culture Paul knew. And look for ways he referenced the culture as he spoke the gospel to those in Athens.

What did you see? Paul felt compelled by God to pursue mission in Athens (v. 16). He knew that there were both Jews and some Gentiles, and he knew where each would be (v. 17). He knew there were philosophers, and that Athenians loved new philosophy (vv.18–21). He knew there was a statue in the Aeropagus to an unknown God (vv. 22–23), and used that fact as a point of connection with share the gospel (vv. 23–31). In the midst of declaring the gospel, he even shows that he knew some of the local culture, quoting Athenian poets (vv. 28). At most, historians think Paul was in Athens for only one winter.[3] How long have you been in your mission field? Did Paul know Athens better than you know your city? Let's follow the example of the greatest missionary in history, and get to know the objective facts and everyday rhythms of our own mission fields.

DAY 12

ANSWER
Everyday missionaries see the ground-level view

READ
John 4:1–30

ZOOM LENS

WE WANTED TO MEET IN THE HEART OF OUR CITY

When The City Church began holding regular Sunday gatherings, we met at Four Day Weekend, a great improv comedy club in downtown Fort Worth. The troupe used their theater on Friday and Saturday evenings, and we got it Sunday evenings. More than once people walked out, realizing we were a church and not the comedy show they had expected. We sang to and talked about Jesus, and we just weren't that funny. We'd wanted to gather in the heart of our city, but here's what we didn't expect: downtown Fort Worth was dead on Sunday evenings. While the downtown was packed with business, life, and commerce every weekday, even Starbucks closed at five p.m. on Sundays! From yesterday's big-picture view, we were in the most strategic location in our city. But once we hit the ground, we realized that the commercial heart of our city was different than its cultural heart. The downtown culture is changing—but at that point, our church learned a lesson and eventually moved our gatherings to a location that better fit our hope of finding the true heart of our city.

While yesterday's big-picture knowledge of our mission fields is helpful for everyday mission, it's only half the story: in order to engage people in meaningful ways, we must learn the ground-level, sub-jective elements too. Bob and I could both know *about* our wives. We could study them; we could learn facts about them; we could even watch their everyday rhythms, as creepy as that sounds. But unless we truly *know* them, we don't have the depth of relationship that marriage should. The same is true of our mission fields: we must swoop down from yesterday's thirty thousand-foot perch, and get to know people, stories, and values, from a ground-level view.

HYPER-LOCAL RHYTHMS

For many of us, yesterday's idea of an entire city is an overwhelm-ing mission field. I grew up in a town of twenty-five thousand peo-ple—a far cry from Fort Worth's nearly million. Even in that small town, there's no way I could pursue mission with everyone. In The City Church, we intentionally shape City Groups around neighbor-hoods; for NorthWood, we focus on neighborhoods but also unique calls that people engage. There's no way one person, family, or even group can reach our entire city. But as God continues to make dis-ciples and we continue to send new groups to new neighborhoods, we join hundreds of other believers and carry out His mission across our city together. Instead of focusing on an entire city, each group focuses on its neighborhood. Coined in a 1991 *Washington Post* ar-ticle, this concept is called "hyper-local."[4]

A hyper-local community is focused on the concerns, shared in-terest, data, and interactions of a well-defined community. Needs, values, trends, and concerns are different, depending on your part of town. In Fort Worth, the lives in upscale, trendy West 7th look different than the minivan-driving, dual-income families who live near better schools south of Loop 820. The daily routine of those scraping by on "homeless row" are wildly different than the artsy, flannel-and-skinny-jeans hipsters of Fairmount, two miles away. Hyper-local mission is likely the reality for an everyday mission-ary. Unless you live in, say, "hyper-rural" Nebraska, are amazing at finding "Persons of Peace" (explained below), or are supernaturally gifted, it's unlikely that you can be a lone ranger missionary to your entire city. Instead, you not only need to learn the statistics of your entire city; you must learn the rhythms of those who comprise your hyper-local mission field.

Here are a few helpful questions from Tim Chester and Steve Timmis, summarized from *Everyday Church*, to help us "get to know our neighborhood, its people, and their stories, values, worldview and culture . . ."[5] Among other questions, they ask:

→ Where are the places and activities we can meet people?

→ Where do people experience community?

→ Are there existing social networks with which we can engage?

→ What are the patterns and timescales [schedules] of our neighborhood?

→ How do people organize their time? When are times we can engage meaningfully?

→ What cultural experiences and celebrations do people value? How might these be used as bridges to the gospel?

→ What sins will the gospel first confront and heal?

→ What is the good news for people in this neighborhood?

HYPER-LOCAL BROKENNESS

My friend Jonathan used to work for the Volunteer Center of North Texas. Before he sent teams to various new areas, they would go through a process of Neighborhood Mapping.[6] Similar to the cross-cultural missionary practice of prayer walking, the goal is seeing things you've never noticed before, looking through the dual lens of brokenness and redemption, and praying for wisdom in knowing how you can best meet needs. Consider the questions below, as you walk (or drive) your neighborhood with others. Ask questions, seek God, and debrief afterward, as you consider ways to redeem the brokenness. Like every other skill, this takes time to develop. Don't feel like you have to be the answer to every question. Simply pay attention to the things God seems to impress upon you:

→ What does God reveal as you notice the type, age, and condition of housing in your area?

→ How many schools exist there? What might God say about some needs they have?

→ What government offices or facilities exist there—including police, fire, etc.? What are ways you might be able to serve, love, bless, or be involved?

→ What kind of businesses are there? What businesses are noticeably lacking? Is God stirring anything in you to help?

→ How safe is it? Are there hazards for children? Is it safe to be out after dark? What might He be calling you to do?

→ What health, social, and human services exist in the area? Is God impressing anything about these to you?

→ What buildings or people does God seem to emphasize in your mind?

→ Be discerning, but what impulses or thoughts might God be giving you?

HYPER-LOCAL GATEKEEPERS

A final thing to look for as you learn your neighborhood is what cross-cultural missionaries call a "Person of Peace." Jesus encouraged His first missionaries to find someone in their mission field whom God had prepared to receive them.[7] Persons of Peace are not just friendly individuals; instead, missionaries throughout history have often spoken of meeting not-yet-believers who not only showed them disproportionate favor, but who proved to be "gatekeepers" to their society, neighborhood, or other mission field. Cornelius, Nicodemus, Gamaliel, and the Ethiopian eunuch are a few among many biblical examples. Each built relationships with and spoke to their tribes on behalf of Jesus and His followers, opening doors for God's gospel work.[8] A local school's librarian is one modern example. She wasn't the principal, but she showed great favor to the Christian teacher we knew, spoke on our behalf to the principal, and we got to serve the school well until she left.

Who are Persons of Peace in your mission field? Who holds the proverbial keys to the neighborhood, school, or company? Maybe it's someone who's more open to discuss faith than you'd expect. Maybe it's the guy who not only seems to know everyone, but is excited to introduce you to his friends. Maybe it's simply the lady with whom you feel a strong connection, who accepts invitations into your life and starts to reveal the depth of hers. It might be the CEO or Neighborhood President, or it might be someone with a lower title, but holds respect and affection in the organization or group. As you learn your mission field, ask God who He's prepared to help along your way.

MAKING THE TRUTH OF JESUS PERSONAL

A hyper-local mission field zooms in from a whole city. But we cannot even leave mission on the communal level; it must get to the level of individual souls. Jesus Himself, the very embodiment of the gospel, shows us how to apply the objective truth of the gospel to a subjective life. When He meets a Samaritan woman in John 4,

101 WAYS
TO DEMONSTRATE THE GOSPEL

36 Travel regular routes: Walk or bike the same route, or take the same public transport each day. Meet others on the same journey; share your story and get to know theirs. Build relationships on your commute.

37 Walk your dog: Walk when your neighbors are outside. Strike up conversations. Invite them over. No dog? Here's your chance to guilt trip your spouse into getting one.

38 Be the kind of neighbor everyone wants: Keep your yard presentable, pick up your dog's mess in #37's walks, and make sure your guests don't block driveways. It's even as simple as waving "hi."

she challenged Him with a question of race and gender roles. Jesus doesn't ignore her question. He doesn't tell her to stop worrying, or that He'll die soon to reconcile the broken socioeconomic status, so she should believe in Him. Not initially. Starting with His need for water, He instead addresses her thirst, both physical and spiritual.

But here's what is often missed: Jesus speaks to something deeper than even spiritual thirst. He speaks to the woman's lack of satisfaction. We see this in her desire to be filled, never having to drink again. We see it as they discuss her string of spouses. We see this in her unfulfilled desire to worship. At every point, Jesus shows Himself—and God's truth—more satisfying than any of her lesser pursuits: water, a man, or worship location. Finally, she declares her understanding of a Messiah who will finally satisfy, and He reveals in verse 26, "I who speak to you am he."

Jesus learned her story. He "met her on her turf." He spoke the objective gospel: "There is a Messiah, coming to free you to worship God in spirit and truth, and I am he!" But He spoke that objective gospel in a way that addressed her personal history. He addressed her felt needs, then pointed to her heart-level need: "God will satisfy you more than THIS." Jesus—Truth incarnate—spoke to her in a personal way. Through this, her life, then other lives through her, were changed.

DAY 13

SHAKEN, NOT STIRRED

IT'S THE UNDERSTATEMENT OF THE MILLENNIUM, OR TWO

ANSWER
Everyday
missionaries
rearrange their
lives for the sake
of others

READ
Acts 9:1–22

In a split-second, a man named Saul's life was changed. He went from making havoc for Christians to preaching Christ. He gave up the prestige and power of Pharisee life, for a life of suffering and making camping gear by night so he could preach the gospel by day.[9] He "confounded the Jews"[10]—of whom he had been a leader and in a sense an employee—to the point they tried to kill him. Many times. In today's terms, it wouldn't be far off to say he went from being a terrorist against Christianity to becoming one of its most prominent leaders.

This is one of the most stark shifts in lives and missions in Christian history, but Paul isn't alone.[11] Four of Jesus' apostles gave up their fishing business to follow Him. Jesus' followers left families for the sake of their faith and mission. A married couple put themselves in danger to house Paul, a wanted fugitive. God's prophets did some crazy stuff, including lying naked by the roadside and eating bread baked with cow poop. Abraham, Rebekah, Joseph, and many others left all they knew for the sake of God's plan. Early churches met in peoples' homes. Early Christians sold their stuff to provide for each other. On and on this list could go, both throughout the Bible and history since.

Some of these situations required people to physically leave homes, relationships, and businesses. There's obviously a re-arrangement of life when people move. If you've ever left town, much less gone into a new state or country, you know how difficult it is to maintain relationships and live by your rhythms. In other scenarios, however, God doesn't call people to physically move, but they no less reorient their lives around His mission. It does no good to get to know our city and neighbors, to learn stats and stories, or on one level, even to pray for our mission field, if we're not willing to do anything about it. So what does an everyday missionary do? We follow the examples of countless Christians around the world and across the centuries: we allow God to rearrange our lives around His mission.

GOD SHAKES UP OUR TIME

Think through a typical week: most of our free time is filled with friends, media, housework, hobbies, meals, events, school ac-tivities, fewer trips to the gym than we'd like, and Bible studies or church events. We said last week that mission *can* happen in our workplaces, schools, neighborhoods, and families. But for it to hap-pen, we must prioritize mission to the point that it determines how, where, and with whom we spend our time. I knew a college student who was in Christian organizations literally five days each week. Between his church, a campus worship gathering, his Christian fra-ternity, and his leadership in a parachurch organization, all his free time was spent in a "Jesus bubble." I know a woman involved with one church, on staff at another, and in no less than three separate Bible studies every week. Those are just two examples among many.

But Bob and I have also seen people leave well-paying jobs where the commute took time away from neighbors, and take lower-pay-ing positions closer to home and spend evenings on mission. We've even seen students take a lower grade on an exam to finish unex-pected conversations with not-yet-believing classmates. These two examples exist among many others. We've both had to personally learn this difficult lesson as well. We have to say "no" to delegate work responsibilities, to quit fun hobbies, to leave space in our weeks for spontaneous interactions, and to know our personal capacities. The same goes for every Christian: do we try to fit God's mission around our priorities, or will we reprioritize our time around God's mission?

GOD SHAKES UP OUR RESOURCES

Even in well-meaning Christian circles, "home" is often promoted as a place of retreat and refuge. Many of us can't wait to turn onto our street at the end of a long day, press a button that opens a wall of our home, drive into our garage, press that button to close out the rest of the world, and enjoy our manicured lawns, backyard oases, and increasingly larger TVs. We're not knocking nice homes, rejecting that God gives gifts for us to enjoy, or denying a legitimate need for rest. We are, however, considering homes as one example—along with cars, clothes, income, and more—in light of Paul's encouragement to the wealthy and Luke's description of using resources for others. "Do good, . . .be rich in good works, . . .be generous and ready to share, thus storing up treasure for themselves as a good foundation for the future, so that they may take hold of that which is truly life." "And all who believed were together and had all things in common. And they were selling their possessions and belongings and distributing the proceeds to all, as any had need."[12]

Have we considered that what we have is Another's? Consider Jesus' parable: "One who is faithful in a very little is also faithful in much, and one who is dishonest in a very little is also dishonest in much . . . And if you have not been faithful in that which is another's, who will give you that which is your own?"[13] Everything we have is a gift from God, to steward on behalf of our Master. Everything we have is a tool for His mission. Our homes, then, are not really "ours," but on loan from God, for God. They're not just a place for personal rest and retreat; that's squandering His resource and claiming it as our own. They're also places for mission, ministry, and relationship. Likewise, our incomes are means by which God supports us to do His work. Since they too are from Him and to Him, our incomes are tools to display God's generosity and blessing to others. The same idea is true for everything we own—or at least, think we own—in our lives.

GOD SHAKES UP OUR RELATIONSHIPS

If rearranging our time and our resources isn't difficult enough, the third thing God often rearranges for the sake of His mission is our relationships. As we've seen, Jesus called His followers to leave homes and families. In much of the world, to become a Christian is to be rejected by those who used to love you. If you're a cross-cultural missionary, you give up relationships for the sake of God's calling. The same is true of everyday missionaries. Each of us only has so many hours, meals, morning bike rides, and weekends to give others. If we say "yes" to everyone, our schedules become too full for mission. If we spend more time with our nuclear family than we should (something very few people would push back on, even if they should), or give precious time to Christians with whom we aren't specifically living on mission (from a church you aren't part of, or outside your mission field), we give away moments that could go to neighbors, coworkers, classmates, and those in need.

We're not suggesting that you cut off every relationship. Rather, reprioritize for the sake of mission. Picture someone filling a bucket with sand, then trying to put large rocks in it: once the sand is compacted, there isn't enough room for the rocks. But if you put the rocks in first, then pour the sand, it easily moves around the rocks, and both fit in your bucket. The smaller grains fit between the larger stones.

That is what it looks like to rearrange your relationships: who are the "rocks" in your life? Who are the people who, in light of God's mission, should rightly fill your weekly "bucket"? Your nuclear family obviously needs quality time, your extended family, roommates, and/or close Christian community must be a priority, as should people you do discipleship with. But those to whom God sent you on mission must be "rocks" too, if you call yourself an everyday missionary. Maybe there are a few others. Who are they? On the other hand, who are the "grains of sand"—the people who need to become secondary; who you may still see, but maybe less occasionally, and only once you've made intentional time for the rocks? Old friends? The old softball team with whom you don't have meaningful friendships anymore? Who else? Maybe they're your sand. And be creative: in what situations can you combine both "making new friends but keeping the old" as it were?

GOD SHAKES UP OUR JOY

This is a tough day: you likely feel a sense of loss; you may be mad at us. But let us encourage you with a final word as we wrap up: on one hand, reorientation takes time. Give yourself grace: two steps forward and one step back—or at times, vice versa—is progress in the battle for your heart. But on the other hand, we're not suggesting these "rearrangings" as arbitrary, legalistic rules. Each of these areas points us to a place we find our joy. We give time, resources, and affection to whatever we find meaning, happiness, and purpose in. If Week One is true—if we're ministers of reconciliation, that

101 WAYS TO DEMONSTRATE THE GOSPEL

39 Designate a "ministry budget": Allot a percentage for mission and ministry in your monthly spending, saving, and giving. It doesn't have to be huge; just the fact that it's there help you use it.

40 Find a new hobby: Not stoked about video games, cycling, or model cars, but know folks who are? Become stoked about people, and prepare to be dominated, out of breath, or have gluey fingers.

41 Move: It's a big commitment, so many readers will immediately write this off. But it's what a missionary does. Where do you have a passion? Pray a ton, get over your fears—and to an extent your logic—and go!

our identity is one of missionaries, and that we're redeemed by God and sent by God—we truly must be "transformed by the renewal of your mind, that by testing you may discern what is the will of God, what is good and acceptable and perfect."[14] Even our thoughts are rearranged. And if we live as everyday missionaries, our basis for joy is too. The gospel of Matthew gives us a simple glimpse of this: "The kingdom of heaven is like treasure hidden in a field, which a man found and covered up. Then in his joy he goes and sells all that he has and buys that field."[15] Joy becomes our motive for a shaken-up life. Rearranging our lives is a sacrifice, but one birthed from waking up to a far greater treasure. Our joy is in Christ, and it's joy that leads us to rearrange our lives, that others may share the same treasure too.

DAY 14

PEOPLE AREN'T PROJECTS

WHAT ARE SOME WORDS CHRISTIANS USE WHEN TALKING ABOUT "EVANGELISM"?

ANSWER
Everyday missionaries grow in love for others

READ
1 Corinthians 12:27–13:8

Often we hear terms like "lost," "sinner," "convert them," "win their souls," "invest in the relationship," or "go after them." From our Christian worldview, some of those terms make sense; some are even pulled from Scripture.[16] But put yourself in the shoes of the person to whom God sent you on mission. How do those ideas—which may be clear in our minds—sound to them? Simply put, the words often associated with evangelism and mission are unnecessarily offensive, if not demeaning, to the very people to whom God sends us. Remember my friend Jerry from the introduction? The reason he wanted to leave lunch is because "every Christian I know just wants to convert me." In any other context, if we try to win something, that thing is a prize to us. And if we invest in anything, we always expect one thing: a return. Without realizing it, our words turn souls into prizes, humans into tallies in a "win column," and relationships into an income to capitalize on.

SPEAK THE TRUTH . . . IN LOVE

First Corinthians 13's "love verses"—the ones heard at every wedding you've ever been to—are actually written in the context of Paul's teaching on spiritual gifts. Some of us have pursued the end of 1 Corinthians 12 and beginning of chapter 13 in the context of Christian community. But let us apply them to everyday mission: with the Corinthians we learn that by God's power, someone can be the greatest evangelist or smartest apologist. They might be the best-versed Bible scholar on earth, or the most lawyer-logical "prover of the gospel." One could have amazing discernment; they might know how to apply the gospel to every unique situation. But if that person doesn't act in love, his earnest efforts are but white noise. His words are radio static; his argument obsolete.

Yes, we must share the gospel. Yes, we must beg for God to change the hearts of those who don't believe in Him as their joy and life. And let us first again affirm that God works through preachers and proclamation, and has uniquely gifted some as evangelists who carry out His work in unlikely situations. But let us at the same time encourage those without these unique gifts: most mission in the Bible happens through meaningful conversations and relationships. People are attracted to genuine friendships. They want to be known; they love to be loved. In everyday situations, over time, in long-term relationships, we demonstrate the natural, normative presence of the gospel. What do everyday missionaries do? We love people well.

PEOPLE ARE NOT PROJECTS

Christians often have no concept of deep friendships with those who aren't Christians. What do we do with people we're close to? We spend time with them. We talk with them. We do hobbies together. We celebrate with them. We even grieve with them. We're in each other's homes often. However it looks, we hang out with them, sometimes without any specific purpose or deeper desire than simply being in each others' lives. When we love people, we spend time with them. This is true of our spouses, families, boyfriend, girlfriend, BFF, and Christian community. Why don't we know how to have that kind of friendship with not-yet-believers, simply because they don't know Jesus?

My (Bob's) daughter Jill helps direct all of NorthWood's community outreach. Her favorite saying is this: "People are not projects." Jerry—and the millions he represents—only know Christians to have an ulterior motive. Yes, we want their best—like we want the best for our believing families and friends. But if every time we're with our not-yet-believing friend, we try to turn the conversation and make sure to throw in salvation—"Man, you broke your leg? You know what else is broken? Your heart. You need Jesus." "Did you see that dunk for the win? That's just like how I felt when God slam-dunked me and won my heart!"—we won't be hanging out much longer.

CONVERSATION AND RELATIONSHIP IN
THE BIBLE AND TODAY

Jesus spent three years with a posse of not-yet-believers. In everyday conversations, object lessons, mediating arguments, and giving miracles and sermons, He slowly but surely demonstrated the gospel.[17] But even after He rose from the dead, it took a while for many to believe. We'll dive into this next week, but Paul reminds the Thessalonians that he and his friends were "delighted to share with you *not only the gospel of God but our lives as well.*" Why? "Because we loved you so much."[18] Even amidst the urgency of his traveling mission, Paul would stay in one place for several weeks or months. He would develop relationships, and over time display and declare the gospel. Even in Philip's road trip with the Ethiopian eunuch—perhaps the briefest evangelistic relationship in Acts—he does not force the gospel uninvited: the eunuch asked Philip into his chariot, and Philip only shared the gospel in response to the eunuch's request to explain his book.[19] We could go on. In each instance, no missionary avoided the gospel. They simply developed at least a conversation, and often a relationship and Christlike love for those they were sent to first. That was the context in which they spoke the gospel.

So again, what do we do with the people we love? Conversations, activities, hobbies, meals, and more. An everyday missionary does those things, regardless of whether the person they're with follows Jesus or not. Because only as we spend time with and truly get to know someone do we develop a true, abiding love for them.

Jimmy said yes to his neighbor's offer to help move Jimmy's family into their new home. After the vans had gone, a few neighbors came over—some Christian, others not—and welcomed the family to the street with food and drink. That initial conversation has now led to three homes with gates in their backyard fences, so families can freely roam into each others' backyards. Many nights of any given week, many people on their block are in a neighbor's home for dinner. The guys on his street buy a keg together every month, and many evenings Jimmy will come home to find neighbors on his back porch, already enjoying the keg, pool, and conversation. These neighbors know each other deeply. Jimmy and Waverlee talk about jobs, marriage, and life with them. And sometimes, they talk about faith. Sometimes they get to pray, whether the neighbors believe in God or not. And they've seen people on their block come to know Jesus. Relationships, love, time, and lots of conversation paved the way.

101 WAYS TO DEMONSTRATE THE GOSPEL

42 Remember birthdays: Other than social media-prompted messages, birthdays are more and more forgotten. Be the one who remembers: a wish, card, or small gift display values and care.

43 Build a backyard campfire: Regularly invite neighbors into your yard. Accompanied by s'mores, crackling late-night fires often open the door for sharing stories and sharing life.

44 Display imperfection: Instead of hiding faults, mistakes, sins, and conflict, talk about your humanness, and the fruit God produces as He continues to redeem it. Our hope can be an answer to their hopelessness.

IF LOVE IS_____, MISSION IS TOO

It was because "God so loved the world, that he gave his only Son . . ." And "we love [others] because he first loved us."[20] We all know verses like this. But do we live them? I (Bob) was at a gathering of global leaders I meet with a couple of times a year. I have become close friends with many of them. I'll never forget when one of the men, a Muslim, came up during a break. He said, "Bob, I know you've read the Qur'an. But I love you very much and care about you. Would you read it again and seriously consider what the prophet Muhammad spoke about? I cannot bear the thought of not being in eternity with you!" He began to cry. *He* was weeping for *my* soul. I hugged and thanked him for loving me so. Then I told him I believe Jesus is the way we find God and I want him in heaven with me too. I loved him enough to tell the truth. I'm confident enough in my faith and Savior that we even agreed to pray for each other.

What does that kind of love look like? Paul explains Christlike love as his letter to Corinth continues. Among other things, it's patient, kind, selfless, humble, truthful, joyful, hopeful, and persistent. If everyday mission is birthed out of love, then everyday mission must reflect the same attributes. If we truly love those around us, and if we truly want what's best for them, our posture is not one of winning souls or gaining a return on an investment. Instead, the posture of everyday mission is one of patience, kindness, selflessness, humility, truth, joy, hope, and persistence. Even when it gets hard, we believe, hope, and endure. Because that's what love does, and mission is birthed by love.

PRAY. A LOT.

MORE THAN CONTROL IT, I HAD TO CONQUER EVERYTHING.

A piece of my vertebrae broke off into a spinal disc in December 2011, shooting constant pain through my back and leg for nearly a year. I lived with a steady diet of spinal injections, Vicodin, physical therapy, and needle treatments in hopes of avoiding back surgery. None worked.

In August 2012, our second daughter was born. A healthy, cuddly ball of laughter now, Maggie's first few months were traumatic. Her doctor called her birth the most difficult C-section she'd seen in her thirty-four-year practice. Then, for a week we gave Maggie five times the proper dose of a medicine due to a pharmacy error. And she was just a harder, fussier baby than her older sister had been. In the midst of joy and thanksgiving that Maggie was alive and healthy, my back pain, medications, and dealing with a difficult baby joined forces with normal new-kid exhaustion and my wife's physical limitations while she healed. And I snapped.

I spent one Saturday afternoon in a crying, yelling, praying rage. Then it hit me: "I hate this because I can't conquer it." Memories flooded back. I realized that since junior high, I'd either become the best at something—leadership, music, even ministry—or I'd quit—like

ANSWER
Everyday missionaries rely on God the Spirit

READ
John 15:1–17

basketball, since I'm what you might call uncoordinated and stopped growing in about third grade. I thought I had figured out parenting a newborn, because in my vast experience of one child, Charlotte had been easy. And I even remember thinking, after yet another failed spinal injection, "Give me the [expletive] needle and I'll just do it myself." For the first time that Saturday, I truly lamented with nineteenth-century pastor Andrew Murray, "As long as I myself am still something, Jesus Himself cannot be everything. My life must be expelled, then the life of the Spirit of Jesus will flow in."[21]

GOD FULFILLS GOD'S MISSION

Many readers approach the mission of God in the same mindset as I approached it in 2012. We rely on our power, rest in our abilities, and trust our devices, words, and knowledge, to carry out God's mission. Or maybe you're the opposite: some distrust our power, doubt our abilities, and feel inadequate in our devices, words, and knowledge. Murray offers the same answer to both mindsets:

It is your part, believer, to deny yourself, to lose your own life, and in the presence of the Lord to sink down in your nothingness and impotence. Accustom yourself to set your heart before Him in deep humility, silent patience, and childlike submission. The humility that is prepared to be nothing, the patience that will wait for Him and His time, and the submission that will yield itself wholly that He may do what seems good is all that you can do to show that you are ready to lose your life.[22]

The most important thing an everyday missionary does is look to God—not ourselves, no matter how highly or lowly we think of ourselves—to fulfill His own mission. In John 15, Jesus invites His followers to "abide in me": we cannot control anything, do any good, or carry out any of God's commands, by our own human power. Detached from our Vine, we are dead branches unable to produce fruit. We're autumn firewood. Only as we rely on the Vine to sustain us by His power, and as we allow God to prune away our sour grapes, does

He bear rich, plump fruit in and through our lives. Jesus gives us two ways we abide in Him, both of which are necessary in mission.

WE KEEP GOD'S COMMANDMENTS, BY GOD'S POWER

The first way Jesus says we abide in Him is to keep His command-ments—specifically to love and to lay down our lives for others. Jesus Himself modeled this better than anyone ever will. But He doesn't leave us to our own ability to follow His example, lay down our lives, and share the love of Christ with others. John 15 ends thus: "When the Helper comes, whom I will send to you from the Father, the Spirit of truth, who proceeds from the Father, he will bear witness about me. And you also will bear witness, because you have been with me from the beginning."[23] In John's previous and next chap-ters, Jesus describes the Helper's work. God the Spirit "will teach you all things and bring to your remembrance all that I have said to you," and put fears at rest. He will "convict the world concerning sin and righteousness and judgment . . . guide you into all the truth, [and] . . . glorify me."[24]

Our reliance on God the Spirit is echoed through the New Testa-ment. Even in this far-too-brief survey, it is clear that God not only calls us to holiness, mission, and obedience; He doesn't even merely model it for us and ask us to follow. Life must flow from the Vine into each branch continually, empowering every moment of the life God calls us to. Only through God the Spirit's power is God the Son "with you always, to the end of the age," enabling the Great Commission. Only though God the Spirit's ability can we exhibit the love, joy, peace, and other marks of Galatians' fruit.[25] Only by God the Spirit do we abide in Christ, and can God carry out His mission through us.

RELYING ON GOD: PRAYER IN EVERYDAY MISSION

The second way we abide in Jesus is to pray. Prayer puts the focus back on the God who sent us in the first place. Instead of relying on facts, strategy, and even logic to know to do, prayer admits that *our* best planning and plotting are not enough for *God's* mission. To know our mission field, we seek God's revelation: more than what *they* think they need, what's *He* have for them? Instead of ways *we've* discovered to meet folks, how would *God* have us engage? God alone chose each of us to bear fruit, but we must acknowledge our dead-branch inability and "ask" the Vine to gush new life into and through us, as we "go and bear fruit." As we pursue mission, we pray for five things:

We Pray for Those to Whom God Sends Us

When is the last time you meaningfully prayed for those God sent you to? Jeremiah reminds us that we not only "seek the welfare of [our] city" but that we also "pray to the Lord on its behalf, for in its welfare you will find your welfare."[26] If we love our mission field and those within it, we pray for its general welfare—grace, favor, and blessing—specifically and by name, often.

We Pray for Spirit-led Discernment

Different situations, circumstances, and objects surround us every day. Many could be the starting point for gospel proclamation as we see it reflects the world's brokenness or God's redemption. But different beliefs, excuses, and emotions also exist in those around us. We pray that God opens doors to share the gospel in normal ways; that He leads us clearly. We pray for the right moment, words, actions, and posture, to display or declare the gospel in the most meaningful way for each person.

We Pray That God Emboldens Us

For even the most confident among us, speaking the gospel is often nerve-racking. We worry about offending them; we worry about misrepresenting God. We pray to God to fill us with the same Spirit who is a Helper and also a Comforter and Teacher. Only God can convict, reveal Himself, give understanding, and change lives. Paradoxically then, as we pray that God gives us the boldness necessary to declare the gospel without fear, we find ourselves in humble reliance on Him.

We Pray That God Softens Hearts

The best gospel proclamation goes nowhere if God the Spirit has not convicted the hearer and softened them to hear the good news. You likely heard the gospel many times before it actually meant something to you. We both did. As we pray for our mission fields, pray that God goes before us, preparing those to receive the good news of God.

We Pray That God Draws People to Himself

Above all, we pray that God will carry out His redeeming work in the lives around us. As He gives us discernment and emboldens us, we must be prepared to play part in God's answer to the prayer. But the most loving prayer we can pray for our neighbors, coworkers, family, and those in need is that God will carry out His redeeming work in their lives, however He chooses to work.

ADMITTING INABILITY

We are no more able to carry out God's mission without God's power, than I was able to heal my own back without the skill and experience of a surgeon—or even to conquer my idol of conquering

101 WAYS TO DEMONSTRATE THE GOSPEL

45 Practice reliance on God: Starting each day in prayer admits a need for God's power. Reading the Bible displays a need to know Him and His character. A journal allows you to confess, repent, and humble yourself.

46 Pray before conversations: Whether a meeting, business call, friendly chat, or first date, pray before it starts, for God to lead your words, help you model His character, and open doors.

47 Practice humility: Humility functionally displays a belief in God's control. Work on your sense of entitlement, desire for justice, and need to be right, and consider others before yourself.

things by my own power. In your pursuit of mission, rely on God the Spirit to do what only God can do. Bathe your mission field in prayer. And, as in every other aspect of life, "deny yourself and follow Him. Lose your own life and find His. Let Him impart Himself in the place you have up to this time retained for your self-life. From there will flow rivers of living water."[27]

"WHAT" QUESTIONS FOR YOU TO WORK THROUGH

☐ **GENERAL**: What impacted you the most this week? What was new, convicting, or confusing? What was difficult? What do you need to discuss with others?

☐ **GENERAL**: Where's your heart, as you consider God's mission? What are you currently thinking? What's motivating you? What scares you? How is God moving in you?

☐ **DAY 11**: What are some of the resources in your community, through which you can find objective facts about your mission field? What are some of the facts you learn?

☐ **DAY 11**: Think of your community as a whole, and work through the "story" questions on page 87. What are some of the themes you notice, and how does it impact their corporate view of the gospel? Do the same for specific people in your mission field.

☐ **DAY 12**: Work through the list of "hyper-local rhythm" questions and "prayer walk" list on pages 92 and 93. It might take you a few days to learn these rhythms, but once you do, what are some themes you saw?

☐ **DAY 12**: Related to the lists on Day 12, look at Stuart Murray's list of shifts in this week's intro paragraphs. What shifts have happened in your mission field, which are happening, and which seem imminent?.

☐ **DAY 13**: What are some ways you regularly give your time to? List some of the resources you have. This is a tough question, but how might God be calling you to rearrange your time and resources for the sake of His mission?

☐ **DAY 13**: Who do you spend time with in a given month? Another tough question, but who should be the "rocks" you prioritize as a missionary, and who should be "sand" to fill in the gaps?

☐ **DAY 14**: What do relationships look like with not-yet-believers? Are you truly growing in Christlike love for them? If not, why is it difficult for you?

☐ **DAY 14**: Considering all the phrases in 1 Corinthians 13:4–8a, what are some of the ways, in your life, that mission can be "patient, kind," and so on?

☐ **DAY 15**: How often have you meaningfully prayed for your mission field? Your coworkers, classmates, not-yet-believing family, and those in need? What things can you start praying for each?

☐ **DAY 15**: What does relying on God the Spirit look like in your life in general? What are some ways it's easy to see your need for His work and power in His mission? What are ways others can help you rely on God more than yourself, for all of life and for mission?

☐ **GENERAL**: Look back over this week's "Everyday Mission Ideas." What additional, practical things can you come up with, specific to your personality, gifting, and mission field, to live out God's mission? Share your ideas online with the hashtag #everydaymission.

MY MISSION

MARK DEYMAZ

LITTLE ROCK, ARKANSAS

Not long after our church, Mosaic, moved into the old Walmart, a homeless man named Raymond began attending faithfully from week to week. Typical of those on the street, he was disheveled, and he often reeked of alcohol. Each Sunday, he would first head for the bathroom to clean up before coming back to get a cup of coffee and sit down.

One morning during the service, I invited the congregation to break up into smaller groups for prayer. As I left the platform, a high school student named Sandra motioned to me. Raymond was sitting close to her, and wanted me to pray with him. I sat and began to talk with him and, more important, to listen. During our brief exchange, Raymond spoke from his heart. He confessed that drugs and alcohol had consumed his life and had left him isolated from family members living nearby. At Mosaic, he said, the people were friendly and treated him

kindly. Coming each week gave him peace and hope. "I feel so good here! I feel the Spirit of God here. I may live bad Monday through Saturday, but I like to come here on Sunday because it makes me feel so good!"

Taking his hands, I prayed for him. And touched by the interaction, I concluded the prayer time by asking Raymond to come forward to share his story. As he spoke, it was evident to all that Raymond desired to be cleansed from his addictions and restored to his family. Having shared from his brokenness and despair, Raymond asked the church to pray for him. In response, about a dozen Mosaics came forward and embraced him warmly. It was the first physical touch or affection he had received in a very long time. Laying their hands upon him, they led the entire church in praying for Raymond that day. It was a beautiful sight to see—the body of Christ extending the love of God to this man who had come "just as I am." There wasn't a dry eye in the house.

In time, some men helped Raymond to enroll in a twenty-eight-day detoxification program. He then entered rehabilitation, and upon completion came by the church as a completely different man. Soon Raymond again stood before the church, this time to ask forgiveness for the times he had taken advantage of generosity. More important, he shared that he had committed his life to Christ. At our last interaction, he had continued in sobriety and held a steady job at a fast-food restaurant.

Others like Raymond soon found their way to Mosaic. With them came needs for basic things such as food, clothing, and medical attention. This led us to stock a small closet in 2004, first with food and then clothing. In time, the needs grew. People needed beds, prescription medicine, treatment for alcohol and substance abuse, and other things we had no systematic way of providing.

In those days we simply asked the body to donate as we became aware of needs, and most of the time our people came through. In time, we began to store such items in order to be more proactively prepared. As word spread, the demand on our time and resources grew exponentially, and required greater organization, more planning, and the involvement of people beyond our staff and membership. Initially assisting some two hundred and fifty people in the first twelve months of this ministry we now call The Orchard, in 2012 we provided free food, clothing, and material goods to 17,564 people from 2,563 unique households in the 72204 zip code. Amazingly, this number represents over 53 percent of the entire population residing in our zip code. Furthermore, since over 21 percent of the population lives in poverty (2,707 households), this means that nearly 95 percent of households in poverty were directly served through The Orchard in 2012.

When a local church is multiethnic and economically diverse for the sake of the gospel, and when it reflects more than the community but rather the kingdom of heaven on earth, then being missional isn't a program to embrace or something you do. It is simply who you are.

MARK DEYMAZ is founding pastor of the Mosaic Church of Central Arkansas. An author and contributing editor for *Outreach* magazine and *Leadership Journal*, Mark serves as the Executive Director of the Mosaix Global Network, an organization dedicated to inspiring unity and diversity in the local church throughout North America and beyond. markdeymaz.com

WHEN DOES EVERYDAY MISSION HAPPEN?

Bob and I are both busy. You're busy. Everybody's busy. How can we possibly add everyday mission to our already-packed fifteen-to-nineteen waking hours of each day? The very thought is enough to overwhelm us and keep us from even trying. But what if that's the wrong question? God's mission cannot be added into our busy lives; our busy lives must wrap around God's mission.

Let us start this week by helping you give yourself grace: there are seasons—of the year of life—where mission looks a bit less active. Folks up north can't throw outdoor barbecues many months of the year. Husbands, don't leave your wife at home and go to the neighbors the day you bring your newborn home from the hospital. Because of a book deadline, this year's Super Bowl was the first I can remember that our house wasn't filled with friends and neighbors—even though ironically, the book is about just such mission! Don't become legalistic. Let's recognize the seasons in our lives, families, work duties, and mission fields. And let's pray: for our mission fields and for discernment to know how to pursue mission well, even as it varies season by season.

At the same time, let's recognize that seasons pass, and that busyness can become an excuse to avoid the difficulty of God's call. Winter turns to spring. That newborn can be a great reason to invite neighbors over. Work settles down—at least for a few moments. And mission can become more active again. Additionally, a little thought and creativity can turn some of those excuses into great opportunities. Here's the starting point for this week: everyone has the same number of hours a day and months in a year. As we ask, "When does everyday mission happen?" the answer begins by considering how we use those God-given hours, days, months, and years.

DAY 16

YOU'RE CRAZY

PEOPLE SHOULD THINK WE'RE LEGITIMATELY CRAZY.

ANSWER
Everyday mission happens when our mission field sees the choices we make

READ
1 Peter
2:11–3:22

Paul tells Christians in Corinth, "If in Christ we have hope in this life only, we are of all people most to be pitied. But in fact Christ has been raised from the dead, the firstfruits of those who have fallen asleep."[1] We *do* have hope, joy, and purpose beyond this life only, because of Jesus' resurrection. If that hope is real to us, then the way we live, the things we spend money on, the choices we make, and everything we do looks different than those in our mission field. When people look at our daily lives and see things like generosity in relative poverty, joy in the midst of pain, the way we forgive and show grace—to even the hardest people in our lives, they shouldn't just see us as a little different from themselves. Instead, Paul is teaching that we should live in a way that makes folks wonder if we've got a few screws loose. They should see such a massive difference that they may even pity us, because they don't get the seemingly illogical, erratic decisions we make. This lifestyle has nothing to do with self-glory or a desire to be seen but is instead the natural response to realizing the life-changing reality of the gospel. Because of Jesus' work in us, our lives, choices, and decisions are marked by gospel abnormality.

ABNORMAL DISPLAYS OF OUR FAITH

What are some abnormal ways we can live? Bob and I know people whose children qualified for scholarships at the finest private school across town, but instead chose to enroll in their neighborhood's public school. They spent time discipling their children through their homework, taking responsibility for their kids' learning. They realized there was no better way to meet their neighborhood than to walk to the same school, join the same PTA, and go to the same events as them. We know folks who sold massive homes, took the tax hit, and bought a smaller home in a rough part of town, to live among those to whom they were called on mission. We know folks who make double the amount of food they need for dinner each night, because their door is always open, and the family never knows exactly how many neighbors and friends will to show up to eat. Adopting, reunifying, and fostering orphans are some of the best reflections of the gospel we can see today. But it goes against cultural norms to bring nonbiological people into our families.

Peter gives a few more glimpses into lives of gospel abnormality. After explaining our right motives in the first one and a half chapters, 1 Peter shows in today's verses how that abnormality plays out in everyday ways. Our view of—and even submission to—human authority looks different from the world around us, because we see God as sovereign. So the way we speak about our national leadership, school policies, or parents should reflect a trust in something deeper. Our marriages look different, because it reflects a deeper covenant. So we commit to a beauty deeper than physical, and we respect, forgive, and show grace to each other, by a power not our own. We suffer differently.[2] God's people found joy in persecution, so surely a stubbed toe or frustrated boss shouldn't ruin our day.

EVERYDAY MISSION IN EVERYDAY CHOICES

We could go on through the rest of Peter's letter, but it follows the same pattern. Earlier in our book we considered our role as priests, and said that we either "proclaim the excellencies of him who called you out of darkness into his marvelous light,"[3] or we proclaim some other hope, joy, and savior. This week we consider when everyday mission happens. We start by seeing normative, everyday life as the context for that functional proclamation: in balanced responses to situations both good and bad, in the illogical way we view gifts God has given us, in our relationships, in the abnormal choices we make, and in all we do, we "proclaim the excellencies of God."

To say it another way, everyday missionaries are called to such a unique, strange life, that there is no way to explain it other than the massive change God has made in us. But here's the catch: in order for people to see the gospel change in us, and even in order for folks to shake their head and say, "Man that guy's weird!" we have to live out our mission in a way that people can see it. So when does everyday mission happen? When the people God sends us to see the choices we make.

Before he starts into examples above of this strange life we live, here are the final words of the foundation Peter builds: "Beloved, I urge you as sojourners and exiles to abstain from the passions of the flesh, which wage war against your soul. Keep your conduct among the Gentiles honorable, so that when they speak against you as evildoers, they may see your good deeds and glorify God on the day of visitation."[4]

There are two extremes to Peter's thought—and most Christians are better at one while ignoring the other. Verse 11 reminds us that we're sojourners and exiles, and as such calls us to abstain from sin. Misreadings of this verse have yanked some Christians out of the world around us. Some Christians read "abstain from the passions of the flesh" as "abstain from being around anyone or anything 'non-Christian'." So they lock themselves away from their city—in a castle with a big cross on the drawbridge so everyone knows it's a Christian castle when it's pulled up—in an attempt to "stay unstained" by the world outside the castle walls. In verse 12, Peter disallows that extremist, removal mindset. Where does God call us to live out that holy life? *Among the Gentiles.* If you're unaware there are Gentiles around, that's simply the biblical term for "everyone who wasn't one of God's people." Rather than keeping faith huddled in holy ghettos, Peter call Christians to live it out in public—in the midst of those who don't follow Jesus.

The other extreme we can slip into goes beyond living our faith among the Gentiles, to instead living *like* the Gentiles. This extreme finds joy, hope, and satisfaction in the same things they do. This is just as dangerous a misinterpretation as the first: it overemphasizes grace and rejects obedience of His radical, culturally pitiable call. The two-sided principle in verses 11 and 12 encourages us to balance those extreme views.

A VISIBLE LIFE AND FAITH

Peter's reason for living out our faith in the midst of not-yet-believers echo Jesus' words in the Sermon on the Mount:[5] "So that they may see your good work and give glory to your Father who is in heaven." On one hand, if we hide in our Christian castle, people

101 WAYS
TO DEMONSTRATE THE GOSPEL

48 Treat those who serve you better than they deserve: The waiters, assistants, janitorial staff, drivers, and housekeepers who surround us, greet them by name. Get off your phone before you check out of a store. Tip well, even if they did a horrible job. Show dignity, kindness, grace, mercy, and the love of Christ.

49 Sit at the bar: Restaurant bars are great places to strike up a conversation. Leave your table or booth, pray that God opens a door, and introduce yourself.

50 Use your business for your community: Bless your shoppers, diners, and those who use your services. Donate to organizations. Through generosity and service, allow people to ask "Why?"

can't see our lives and glorify God because they can't see our lives, period. We must put down the drawbridge and live out our faith in public. On the other hand, if in our decisions, choices, actions, and very lives people can see no discernible difference that Jesus has made in us, versus the lives of others—people can't see our lives and glorify God because our lives and deeds aren't proclaiming the glory of God.

Everyday mission happens when our goals, time, resources, decisions, and day-to-day lives functionally proclaim what we mentally affirm. When can people see the great change God makes in us, and when can they and we glorify God in it? Often, it happens in the natural, spontaneous moments of daily life. That's what we look at tomorrow. But today's answer is that those natural, spontaneous moments of gospel display happen in the midst of such a unique, abnormal lifestyle, that there is no way to explain it other than the massive change God has made in us.

REDEEM THE BORING

DAY 17

JESUS WAS QUITE THE BUSY MAN.

In today's context, we would call Him an itinerant minister, preaching and healing from place to place, among sometimes unsuspecting people. His calendar was full of meetings, sometimes with an array of unsavory people. At least some days He rose early to pray and prepare for His day, and was at least occasionally up late. He was often interrupted by spontaneous conversations, children, and angry detractors, who He seemed to make time for, even if it was not convenient. He dealt with public firestorms and backlash. Then He would head to another group and start all over again.

For someone who's often depicted as so serene, this is how Jesus spent the whole thirty-six-or-so months of His whirlwind public ministry. In the midst of His busy life, the Gospels show us four activities that Jesus did often. Each is encapsulated in today's reading:[6]

1. Walking: Much of Jesus' time was spent on the road. He didn't go far from his home, but traveled from nearby city to nearby city, taking His seemingly random band of followers with Him. On the way, they argued, asked questions, argued, stopped to rest, argued, served Jesus, and argued some more. Whether with twelve

ANSWER
Everyday mission happens in ordinary moments of life

READ
Matthew 14:13–33

or seventy-two or more people, many of Jesus' stories and much of His nonpublic teaching happened as He walked.

2. Working: Jesus spent much time carrying out "nothing of his own accord, but only what he sees the Father doing."[7] He did so by displaying and declaring restoration, new life, love, and true *shalom*. In teaching, healing, defending Himself, performing miracles, raising from the dead, correcting misperceptions, and more, Jesus did His job well.

3. Eating and drinking: Especially in Luke's gospel, we see Jesus eat and drink often: with tax collectors, sinners, and prostitutes; with the four thousand and the five thousand; with the religious elite and the poor; with His disciples. And let's not forget His first miracle, creating lavish libation for a wedding party. Meals, water, and wine were the subject of some parables. And much of Jesus' ministry, and many significant events in His life, occurred in the context of food and drink.

4. Praying: Both publicly and privately, Jesus prayed often. We see Him praying early in the morning, late at night, in front of many people, and with a few. We've already considered prayer as one of the marks of an everyday missionary. But we're convinced the reminder cannot be overstated: the Son of God spent a lot of time with His Father.

COMPARTMENTALIZATION VS INTEGRATION

Jesus' activity is helpful as we consider our own. It's especially helpful to see that most of what Jesus did, He did with others. Yes, there are glimpses of Him walking alone. A few times He sent everyone ahead and caught up later—once via an evening stroll on the sea. And we see Him praying in solitude. But not always. More often, Jesus walked, worked, ate, drank, and even prayed alongside and in the midst of His disciples, the outcasts of society, and those in need. And while this is easy to miss, if He did these things with others, then He did them with folks who weren't Christians. Because at the time, that was His only option.

What's the difference between Jesus and us? One, we're not God. But two, Jesus integrated ministry and mission into daily life, while nearly everyone we know—including ourselves—defaults to the opposite. We compartmentalize ministry into certain times and activities, separate from the rest of our lives. If we're not careful, "mission" is relegated to a Saturday morning time slot. We do nice things, check our watches often, then wrap up and go to Chili's. Saturday morning we go do mission, Saturday at noon we go to lunch. Or we have a certain evening for our Bible study group to come watch a movie, but if a coworker asks us to hang out, we make up an excuse and try to take a rain check. We have "Christian friend nights" and "not-Christian friend nights." And so on. This easy mindset rejects the fact that we *are* missionaries, and relegates "mission" back to something we either do or don't, or something we merely do then stop doing in order to do something else.

Mission is not alone; this follows the pattern of Western life: we have work or school hours, social time, a church block, our weekend chunk of time, and so on. When we started The City Church, we introduced people to new identities God gives us in the gospel: in Christ, we are disciples of God, members of God's family, and missionaries to God's world. Before we knew how to flesh those out well, many folks became very busy, planning separate events each week for each: discipleship nights, then family nights, then mission nights. We followed the compartmentalization we were used to. When friend and missionary Caesar Kalinowski was in town, he noticed that this separation made us too busy: we were doing many things—some good—but it was wearing us out.

REDEEMING EVERYDAY MOMENTS

What's the solution to compartmentalized, overly busy mission, in the midst of our compartmentalized, overly busy lives? Our intentionally cheesy answer to ask, with bracelet-wearing church kids of the 1990s, "WWJD?" Jesus didn't compartmentalize; He didn't try to fit ministry in between His "job." He didn't even seem to have specific events for one type of people, then other events for others.

From rich to poor, from the Hebrew Law's "clean" to "unclean,"[8] and from doctor to fisherman, Jesus integrated people, life, ministry, and mission. He redeemed the everyday, normal moments of His life and used them for God's mission. As we try to do the same, we can likewise redeem everyday moments and integrate mission into our ordinary lives.

What things do you do every day of the week? What classes do you take or teach every week of the month? What events do you attend every month of the year? There are normal, ordinary, sometimes even boring moments in our lives that can be redeemed for God's mission. Here are just a few of the most common, redeemable moments:

→ We eat about twenty-one meals a week: sometimes less, sometimes a few more than we should.

→ Many commute to and from work or school, or take children to and from school.

→ Lots of people do yard work or other chores on Saturday mornings.

→ Depending on where you are in the nation, you might play in your yard many evenings, or go for a stroll around your neighborhood.

→ Every fall, football fans find themselves in front of a TV between Thursday until Monday, for either college or pro games.

→ If you don't like football, you end up on the couch for your favorite reality show, comedy, or drama.

→ You likely eat out, at least occasionally.

→ You do something like going to the gym, getting your hair cut, oil changed, or car washed, or having nails done or tattoos redone.

→ You have hobbies: whether movies, train-spotting, music, hiking, surfing, baking, or even gaming, many can involve others.

→ Someone in your home goes to the grocery store, at least once every couple of weeks—and other errands require you to walk, ride, or drive as well.

→ Many families go on at least a vacation or two each year.

MISSION IN EVERYDAY LIFE

Everyone in your mission field does many of these things, just like you. Each of these moments—and so many more—are chances to weave mission into everyday activities or life. Carpool to work or school, or walk, or take public transportation. Invite neighbors over to watch the game you're both planning to watch. Meet your co-workers for breakfast, even if only once a month. Set up play dates for your kids' classmates, with both Christians and those who aren't. Would you ever consider even vacationing with another family?

Just like Jesus did, we each travel, work, eat and drink, and hope-fully pray. Each day is filled with ordinary moments and activities, which we often do alone, or with a certain "type" of friend. But even

101 WAYS
TO DEMONSTRATE THE GOSPEL

51 We eat twenty-one meals each week: Eat as many of those with folks in your mission field as you can. Go out with them; invite them over. Skip the sack lunch once or twice a week, and eat with others.

52 Watch the game together: Pro football happens every Sunday and Monday. Even better, college ball happens Thursday through Saturday. Find a team to root for, or watch that week's rivals.

53 Don't like football? Pick your favorite sitcom, drama, or reality show, and throw a watch party every week. Why watch alone, or with only other Christians, when many others will watch it too?

54 Hang out in your front yard and porch: Play, cook, hang out, and live where others have access to you. Many of us remember the good old days when this was the norm; re-create that culture.

the simplest of activities is an opportunity for worship and mission: "Whether you eat or drink, or whatever you do, do all to the glory of God."[9] When can we integrate life and mission? Rather than segregating people into different time slots or adding things to busy schedules, everyday mission happens when we redeem everyday moments.

SHHHHHH . . .

DAY 18

A MAN WALKED INTO A COFFEE SHOP . . .

It sounds like the start of a joke, but this one's true. A man walked into a coffee shop, sat at the first table, and put a sign on his table: "Free coffee if you listen to my story." He sat for an entire day, and had zero takers. He returned the next day. Same coffee shop, same table. But a new sign: "Free coffee if you *tell me* your story." Again he sat all day. But this time, he had such a response there was a line to his table bringing coffee to him, and he had to beg for a couple of restroom breaks. Even without reading this story, the principle is ingrained in us: we need to be known, heard, and understood. If that's true of us, it's true of those to whom God sends us.

PATIENCE AND LISTENING

Christians aren't known for our ability to listen. Unless of course, it's a podcast of our favorite preacher. When it comes to different faiths or beliefs, the common perception is that we don't care, and only listen in order to find opportunities to shoot their side down. If, as we said last week, mission is compelled by love, then we must embrace listening as one of the most loving things we can do.

Alongside listening—even the motivation for listening—is patience. As much as we're not

ANSWER
Everyday mission happens when we patiently listen

READ
1 Corinthians 3:5–11

known for listening well, Christians certainty aren't known for patience with folks we disagree with. A guy I knew in college stated this evangelistic strategy: "I'll meet with them twelve times, then if they're not a Christian, I drop 'em and move on." He was proud of it; he made it known among his Christian friends. He would even prooftext Jesus' words to His disciples about shaking the dust from their feet if an entire town rejected them. That saying, in three of the four gospels,[10] has some truth. And maybe there's a time to leave a relationship, but certainly it's not after a preset number of official evangelism meetings. If people are people, not projects, the twelve-meeting program is certainly a loss.

On the opposite end of the spectrum, how long did God pursue you? How long was He patient? Maybe He redeemed you when you were six years old. Even that young, He pursued you for *six years* on earth—after knowing you from eternity past. For many of us, the realities of God, faith, and redemption didn't become real until far later in life. My mom was in her thirties and my dad his forties when God redeemed them. Now, a couple of decades later, they spend much of their free time building relationships, sharing life, and reflecting the God who didn't write them off, especially to retired couples who long ago wrote off God. What if God had taken the approach of the guy at college—with my parents, with you or me, or with those to whom He sends you on mission?

LOOKING OUT FOR #1?

Last week we saw some of the marks of Christlike love. Impatience and lack of listening are the opposite of love: they are not kind; they are both arrogant and can be rude. They always insist on their own way. They do not bear, believe, hope, and endure all things. Think about listening and patience in a different context of life: assuming you've ever been "in love," you know well that you want to know that person. You want to learn their joys, passions, and brokenness. You ask questions; you answer theirs. You listen carefully; you discuss and even debate. You enjoy each other. In that scenario, no one accuses you of being false, manipulative, or having an agenda: you truly care about them. The danger of a more practical book, as we mentioned in the introduction, is that some readers will walk away from today saying, "I'm going to listen, because I have to." The reason we listen to people we love is just that: we love them. We want to know their heart and mind; we want to get to their depths. The more we value and respect someone, the more we listen.

Each of us is bent toward pride. So in dating, marriage, parenting, and even friendship, it's hard to "do nothing from selfish ambition or conceit, but in humility count others more significant than yourselves. Let each of you look not only to his own interests, but also to the interests of others."[11] It's hard in much of life. But in mission, it's rarely even considered. Listening and patience put others first.

You might argue, "What's best for them is Jesus. So I want to tell them about Jesus at any cost." Neither of us would disagree that whoever they are, Jesus is the best thing for them. But it requires a life to help them see that, not just words. Once when a homeless person NorthWood was working with decided to get off the streets, the first to jump in was a person who had also been homeless. They didn't want to just receive; they wanted to live on mission. That story had a profound impact on many in the church. It changed the way we saw people. We start where people are and we let the Holy Spirit change them. We may think, even subconsciously, that we are better than others, or we just need to help them, or we have to get them on their feet. As we listen, learn stories, and pay attention, we cannot help but define community beyond those we serve with. It also includes the very people we're serving.

WHOSE TIMING?

"Patience vs impatience" is one of the most common themes in the Bible: Abraham waited decades for a son, and just before God fulfilled His promise, Abraham's impatience led him to take matters into his own hands. Moses got impatient with Israel, and let his frustration show many times during their forty-year wandering. It took Joseph at least a half century to declare that God used his abusive family, jealous boss' wife, and forgetful servants for his good.[12] Jesus' disciples, on the other hand—especially Peter—had no idea what they were asking when they begged Jesus to inaugurate the kingdom sooner than God planned.[13] But they had to wait. Old Testament prophets and New Testament disciples endured persecution, imprisonment, and pain for the sake of God's mission.[14]

It's no surprise that a short consideration of those who do not wait on God's timing in the Bible end up on a poor path: Isaac and Ishmael introduced a history-long quarrel; Moses lost his ticket to the Promised Land; Jesus' disciples got rebuked; and so on. But we also see the blessing of those who wait on God's timing. The disciples entered into "the joy of [their] Master" for their patient endurance; Abraham and Moses were counted faithful. And of course Joseph's words echo great truth: "You meant evil against me, but God meant it for good."[15]

Everyday mission is an opportunity to take matters into our own hands, or to trust God. Will we take matters into our own hands, or

101 WAYS
TO DEMONSTRATE THE GOSPEL

55 Ask good questions: Show them you care about them, their beliefs, and their desires. "When do you feel like that?" "Were you afraid?" "How did you respond?" "What concerns you most?" "How are you doing with it now?" "Tell me more . . ." and of course, "Why?"

56 Follow up: Anyone can fake listening while the conversation is happening; you show people you actually care by remembering, praying, and following up a week later.

57 Plan more time than you think you need: Don't interrupt, don't glance at your watch. Be willing to go long, for the sake of an unhurried, truly deep conversation.

patiently play whatever part God has for us? We'd be wise to learn from Paul's own experience. In today's verses, Corinthian Christians gave both him and Apollos too much credit. But Paul didn't allow them to celebrate either man or give them credit for God's work, but rather pointed toward God, who alone redeems and causes growth.

Ours is not to save, nor determine the timing or relationship in which God draws people to Himself. Maybe we lay a foundation for someone else to build upon; maybe we build upon a foundation someone has previously laid. Maybe—rarely—we get to see both. But "no one can lay a foundation other than that which is laid, which is Jesus Christ."[16] In the big picture of God's history, it doesn't matter if we get to see God redeem someone or if we're just part of the process. God's role is to save. As His workers, our role is to be patient, listen, obey God, and love people. Then we walk through doors as He opens them. But God alone gives growth, whether in one day, six months or forty years. Either way, it's His timing, not ours.

DAY 19

BETTER TOGETHER

FROM HOLMES AND WATSON, TO LUCY AND ETHEL, TO THE AVENGERS, MISSIONS HAPPEN BEST WITH OTHERS.

Whether solving mysteries, creating comical antics, or saving the world from super-villain alien gods, these teams give us a glimpse into the best way any mission is carried out: in community. We see this all around us, every day: a business's mission is to sell a product and turn a profit, so their team comprises salespeople, accountants, marketing, and delivery departments. Everyone plays his or her part to accomplish the mission. If every baseball player on the field is a first baseman, the other team is sure to win.

Bob and I are "big-picture" thinkers, so we gave the draft of this book to editors who see it from a different angle for pushback, then to detail thinkers to make grammar and punctuation "more good." Designers, sales and marketing teams, friends, and of course, each week's storytellers all came together to make the book better. Other than iconic, individualistic rebels like James Bond or Jason Bourne, most mission—in any context of the word—happens better with others. The same has always been true of Christian mission: from the first Christian missionaries in the Bible, to cross-cultural teams on mission, to everyday mission, mission is designed to be shared.

MISSIONAL COMMUNITY IN THE BIBLE

We're hearing more and more about "missional community" in Christian circles. Like any buzzword, its meaning changes—or is lost—depending on who says it. Some missional communities are simply rebranded Bible studies. Others are weekly meetings with little interaction otherwise. But the biblical model for missional communities is neither of these. The New Testament shows us literal communities of Christ-followers devoted to Christ's mission. And as they went into their mission field, they were sent together. Two gospels record the method by which Jesus sent out His first missionaries: both "the twelve" and "the seventy-two" went out "two by two."[17]

Sometimes—if not often—mission is carried out in *unlikely* community. Highlighted in movies and literature, people with seemingly opposite personalities, who don't get each other, or who even disdain each other, realize that truly, "the whole is greater than the sum of its parts."[18] And they join together to make their mission stronger. Jesus' first two sendings weren't isolated events; throughout the New Testament, we see unlikely bands of people, with varied backgrounds and places in life, serving together on mission.

At various points, Paul (ex-Jew, ex-Pharisee, single, traveling teacher) served on mission with Timothy (mixed-race, raised by mother and grandmother, religious upbringing), with Aquila and Priscilla (married, Jewish converts, Roman exiles, tent makers), with Barnabas (island-dwelling Jewish convert), with Luke (Greek doctor, educated, writer), with Gaius (new believer from Ephesus), and with Lydia (wealthy single woman, Greek, new believer from Philippi), among others.[19] Jesus' first apostles consisted of Peter, Andrew, James, and John (Jewish fishermen, brothers; Andrew left another ministry to follow Jesus); Matthew (despised tax collector, worked for "the man"), Simon (member of radical religious sect, hated "the man" and especially tax-collectors—see where this gets messy?), Philip and Bartholomew (Galilean friends about whom little is known, other than Bartholomew was a skeptic), another James and Thomas (little known, except that James was given the unfortunate nickname "James the less" and Thomas doubted), Judas Iscariot (the traitorous accountant), and one with an identity crisis (called in various places, Thaddeus, Jude, another Judas, and Lebbaeus).[20] We even see community in the Father, Son, and Spirit: equal in authority and "God-ness," each member of the Godhead plays a unique role in the work and mission of God.

WHY MISSIONAL COMMUNITY TODAY?

Both Bob and I believe that little has changed from Jesus' time regarding the priority of mission occuring in community. In a post-enlightenment, post-Christendom society, the Church—neither a building nor an event, but God's people on God's mission together—better demonstrates the gospel than one person ever could. Longtime missionary and theologian Lesslie Newbegin goes as far as to say that for many, "the only hermeneutic of the gospel is a congregation of men and women who believe it and live by it."[21] In other words, especially for people who won't walk into a church gathering, read a Bible, or grab a Christian book, the best way they can see and interpret the gospel and faith (the "only hermeneutic") is seeing how Christians interact together.

We aren't saying that inviting people into our Bible studies, weekly meetings, or home groups should replace inviting them to a Sunday church gathering. We're suggesting involving them in the everyday life of your community. We demonstrate the gospel's Christlike love as we fight, repent, and forgive over dinner. They see generosity as we lend each other clothes, cars, and furniture. They see gratitude and praise as we thank God for meals and credit Him with our joys. They learn right grieving as we surround each other and remain faithful in the midst of pain.

Jesus Himself said that Christians must be known by our love for one another. Church families have the unique opportunity to put that love on display, together. And Newbegin gives a glimpse of why communities are vital to our mission: "Jesus . . . formed a community. This community has at its heart the remembering and rehearsing of his words and deeds . . . [The community] exists in him and for him. He is the center of its life. . . Insofar as it is true to its calling, it becomes the place where men and women and children find that the gospel gives them the framework of understanding, the "lenses" through which they are able to understand and cope with the world."[22]

WHO SHARES YOUR MISSION FIELD?

My City Group lives near TCU's campus—about twenty diverse people live within two sqaure miles of each other. Half of those are students, with varied backgrounds, majors, beliefs, and directions in life. The other half is currently comprised of a cardiologist, a filmmaker, a marketing executive, a few in various roles at TCU, an actress, a waiter/actor-to-be, and some full-time moms. Some are single; some married; others will be soon. One family has four kids, while our college guys have no idea what to do with kids. There's no logical reason we should spend time together. But because of our connection in Christ and our proximity to each other, our City Group is in each others' lives and homes often throughout each month. We

101 WAYS
TO DEMONSTRATE THE GOSPEL

58 Practice the Tom's Shoes principle: Instead of buying a $100 pair of jeans, buy a $50 pair and use the other $50 for a cause: clothes for someone else, an organization you support, etc.

59 Don't segregate: Hang out with folks, regardless of their faith or unfaith. Let them meet each other, find common interests, laugh together, maybe even offend each other, and enjoy the time.

60 Encourage others: Set a goal to compliment things others do each day. Often the first idol to overcome is simply "me"—encouragement is a great way to force yourself to notice others.

eat, play, and have deep conversation together. We give both good and bad advice to each other. We rejoice and mourn together. We point each other toward Jesus. And we love each other.

So when I meet a student I have in class, I don't take sole responsibility for mission with them. Per university policy, it would be borderline creepy to seek too much one-on-one time, or to invite them to my house often. And understandably so. But I can introduce them to students in my City Group who can build more natural relationships in dorms or on-campus. When a premed student walks in, I have little in common with him but he can have an automatic connection with Brendan, our doctor. And so on. My City Group shares a common mission field: our shared neighborhood and the university in it. By our gifts, personalities, experiences, and places in life, we're a messy, unlikely team of missionaries, stronger together despite our differences.

What other followers of Jesus share your mission field? Who lives on your block, works at your office, goes to your school, sends their kid to the same school as yours, has the same interest as you, or even lives in your otherwise not-yet-believing family? In other words, with whom are you sent "two by two," into your mission field? Who is your unlikely team, and how do your differences serve God's mission? These are essential questions to answer, because everyday mission happens best when it's carried out in the context of community.

THE MOST WONDERFUL TIME(S) OF THE YEAR

DAY 20

OCTOBER 31 MAY BE THE MOST DEBATED DAY OF THE YEAR.

For some Christians, it embodies a great clash of faith and culture. Much of our culture celebrates Halloween. While the word means "holy evening," the day has developed a somewhat, um, different reputation. But October 31 is also the day Martin Luther nailed his 95 Theses to the door of a Wittenberg cathedral, sparking the revolution that has divided Protestants and Roman Catholics since AD 1522. So for at least some, October 31 isn't Halloween; it's Reformation Day.

This annual showdown between costumed devils roaming the streets vs modern-day monks hiding in indignation is simply the clearest picture of a question we ask several times each year. How should Christians—on mission to the world who celebrates around us—view holidays? Is it possible they can be of some good? Is Santa *really* an anagram for Satan, or could that be a coincidence? What's the balance of honoring our nation and those who died for our freedoms, and rejecting nationalism because "our citizenship is in heaven?"[23] Can we celebrate another year of life with cake and presents, *and* make that celebration about God's work in that life? With a

ANSWER
Everyday mission happens on holidays and special occasions

READ
Leviticus 23:4–44

little planning and intentionality, holidays and special occasions are great opportunities to seek the glory of God and the good of those to whom He's sent us.

IN THE THIRD BOOK, GOD CREATED HOLIDAYS

Cultural celebrations are not man-made institutions. Like much of God's creation, holidays can be—and have been—distorted for all sorts of less-than-holy purposes. But seen throughout the Old Testament, and most clearly in Leviticus 23, God commanded His people to pause several times each year, simply to feast and celebrate. Here are far-too-brief summaries of Old Testament Israel's national holidays:[24]

→ The Festival of Trumpets (Rosh Hashanah) kicked off the Jewish New Year with the blast of a ram's horn. God's people gathered as one, as Israel kicked off each year with ten days of feasting, celebrating God, and ceasing work to rest in Him.

→ The Day of Atonement was an annual reminder of Israel's sin and God's forgiveness. In a solemn service on the most important day of the Jewish year, one ram was killed as a symbol of appeasing God's wrath, as another symbolized God's removal of sin, being sent into the wilderness never to return.

→ The Feast of Booths saw Israel praying for her upcoming harvest. To visibly recall God's past deliverance from Egypt, they lived in tents for a week. As they then returned to their homes—seventeen days in total after gathering for Rosh Hashanah—they celebrated God's gift of their permanent dwellings, symbolic of His giving them the Promised Land.

→ Passover remembers the biggest event in Israel's history: God's original rescue of His people, in His plaguing power over Egypt. Israel sacrificed and roasted a lamb, and still tangibly recall God's work through readings, foods, and glasses of wine.

→ Passover kicked off the Feast of Unleavened Bread. For seven days, Israel recalled the speed with which their ancestors fled Egypt the night of the original Passover.

→ The First Fruits Offering marked the beginning of the harvest. A day of thanksgiving, the celebration included offering Israel's best produce to God, and recalling God's power and grace in sustaining and providing for His people.

→ The Feast of Weeks (called Pentecost) again pointed to God's provision. Another offering made; more feasts occurred; more thanks shared—this time at the end of the wheat harvest.

BUT I'M NOT JEWISH

This is more than a bit of Jewish history. Each feast foreshadows God's work in Jesus' death and resurrection. These celebrations were celebrated by Jews for centuries and by Jesus Himself. And they inform our own celebrations. First, Leviticus 23 shows that God instituted intentional celebration into the annual rhythm of His people. God's people ceased from work and partied. They cooked meat—a luxury in those days—and enjoyed good drink. They made music, relaxed, and played together. They laughed and grieved together. Celebrations are right and good.

Celebrations also cut to the heart of mission: God's people didn't celebrate by themselves. They included those around them. Even people with different beliefs. Consider this instruction: "You shall rejoice in your feast, you and your son and your daughter, your male servant and your female servant, the Levite, the sojourner, the fatherless, and the widow who are within your towns."[25] This idea echoes through the Old Testament Law: "sojourners" were foreigners in Israel who joined the feasts; "servants" from various nations celebrated with God's people; "strangers" and "aliens" weren't Israelites but joined their events.[26]

A final Levitical lesson is that people, events, and even milestones themselves were never the focus of Israel's celebrations. Israel celebrated one thing, in many ways throughout each year: God. They didn't celebrate *grain*; they celebrated the *Giver* of that grain.

They didn't celebrate *their* power over Pharaoh; they had no such power! They celebrated *God's* power. These lessons combine to show us that not only were not-yet-believers invited to Israel's feasts; they observed—and in ways, even participated—as God's people celebrated God, on days God created for just that occasion.

HOLIDAYS, BIRTHDAYS, AND OTHER OPPORTUNITIES

If Israel—geographically set apart from the rest of the world—publicly celebrated God in the midst of strangers, foreigners, and sojourners, there's hope for us as we consider holidays. God didn't invent Halloween, and Jesus wasn't born on December 25. But these and other annual days have been carved into our culture, to cease work, celebrate, and engage others. Most of the year a neighbor might think you crazy if you show up on their doorstep and demand dessert. But on Halloween it's not just allowed; it's expected. Gifts abound in December, giving us an easy chance to surprise coworkers and classmates with cookies or a brief note. Like Israel, the United States sets aside a day for giving thanks, and the world still rings in the New Year with far more pomp than a trumpet blast. These thoughts impact other special occasions too. We each celebrate our very lives once a year—with at least a birthday greeting on Facebook. And how many stories have we heard, of God redeeming people in the midst of—and maybe because of—the pain and grief of a funeral? Some of the best chances for mission involve inviting our mission field into our special occasions, and joining theirs.

Chris and Sawyer catered in fajitas on Halloween, inviting neighbors to celebrate together. They gave good food and drink to adults on a day known for good candy for kids, then a swarm of bumblebees, dancers, super heroes, and parents trekked the neighborhood together. Kathy gave a toast for Camp's birthday in a crowded restaurant at a table of people of many beliefs, celebrating not only the great husband and dad he is, but the Savior and Spirit he reflects and worships. Many families in The City Church open their Thanksgiving table to international students who can't travel home. They serve the traditional feast and introduce the idea of giving thanks.

They share the gospel as they explain that as Christians, we believe that every good gift echoes the best gift, Jesus. Then they go around and everyone shares something they're thankful for. Most everyone in our context grills out for Labor Day, Memorial Day, and July 4. And Mexican descent or not, many Texans celebrate Cinco de Mayo with tacos and beer.

REDEEMING SPECIAL OCCASIONS FOR GOD'S MISSION

Instead of celebrating these and other occasions alone or with just-Christian friends—and instead of creating "Christian" versions of special events already happening in our city and neighborhood— let's celebrate these occasions on mission. Let's display the gospel through generosity, grace, conversation, and joy. And let's declare the gospel through stories, toasts, and prayers. Sure, many cultural celebrations have long forgotten God. But we haven't, and we've been sent to those who have. God is sovereign, over birthdays, death, and even the fact that someone declared certain days holidays. God uses even the most broken things—and days—for His mission.

101 WAYS TO DEMONSTRATE THE GOSPEL

61 Throw a Super Bowl party: Everyone watches at least this one game every year. Apply this principle to the World Cup, Oscars, or season premieres. Cultural events can be used for mission.

61 Invite people to life celebrations: Birthday parties, weddings, and other life events are great times to bring friends together. Find ways to mention that God is the center of your celebration.

63 Invite people to Thanksgiving and Christmas: The holidays can be lonely; bring people into your celebrations and give them the chance to experience love and blessing.

64 Tell true stories of cultural celebrations: Recite the Christmas story to your extended family. Tell the story of St. Patrick around Irish pub grub. Host an egg hunt in a way that tells the story of Easter.

"WHEN" QUESTIONS FOR YOU TO WORK THROUGH

☐ **GENERAL**: What impacted you the most this week? What was new, convicting, or confusing? What was difficult? What do you need to discuss with others?

☐ **GENERAL**: Where's your heart, as you consider God's mission? What are you currently thinking? What's motivating you? What scares you? How is God moving in you?

☐ **DAY 16**: Which is more tempting for you: living in a Christian bubble or living no differently than not-yet-believers? Why? How do both hinder people from seeing your life and glorifying God?

☐ **DAY 16**: What are some practical ways you can live out your faith "among the Gentiles" in your specific context, life stage, and mission field—even if those ways look abnormal?

☐ **DAY 17**: Make three columns, labeled "daily," "weekly," and "monthly." Write as many specific activities as you can think of—no matter how glamorous or boring—that you do regularly in each time frame.

☐ **DAY 17**: Looking back at your list, what are ways that you can incorporate others into some of those normal, everyday moments?

☐ **DAY 18**: Do you see those in your mission field more like people or projects? For either, in what tangible ways do you show them your view of them?

☐ **DAY 18**: What are proactive ways you can be more patient and listen better, to those God has sent you on mission?

☐ **DAY 19**: Who are people in your Christian community with whom you share a mission field? For each, what are some of their unique gifts, experiences, stages of life, etc.?

☐ **DAY 19**: What are some things you can do outside of church or Bible study events to introduce not-yet-believers in the life of your Christian community?

☐ **DAY 20**: Think through the holidays we celebrate each year. What elements of God's character or His gospel work does each holiday reflect? What are some aspects of each holiday that can spark a conversation about Jesus?

☐ **DAY 20**: What are specific ways you can invite not-yet-believers into your holiday celebrations and special occasions—even if it takes changing your traditions or sacrificing your comfort?

☐ **GENERAL**: Look back over this week's "Everyday Mission Ideas." What additional, practical things can you come up with, specific to your personality, gifting, and mission field, to live out God's mission? Share your ideas online with the hashtag #everydaymission.

MY MISSION

STEVE TIMMIS

SHEFFIELD, UNITED KINGDOM

I have to confess a bias toward a particular kind of mission. For me, it's corporate all the way. I don't despise so-called personal evangelism: the fact that the Lord could save an African aristocrat through the solitary witness of an itinerant evangelist who just happened to pop up alongside his moving sedan, should temper my preference. I remember being convicted at a very young age by the

retort of D. L. Moody to a critic of his evangelistic methods: "Better the evangelism I do than the evangelism you don't." But, nonetheless, my bias toward corporate mission remains. This is pragmatic, but it flows out of profound theological principles I won't rehearse here. Exposing people to a diverse community of ordinary people in the process of being transformed by the grace that is theirs in Christ in the messiness of life cannot be anything but good. So the mundane and the ordinary excite me, because that is where the gospel is sown, grows, and bears fruit.

Take Josh. We've known him for quite a few years. His relationship with the gospel has not been altogether straightforward. At times he seemed so far away. His life was a mess, and his decisions foolish. Other times he seemed soft and receptive. But no real progress was made. But Christians kept loving and serving him, and picking up the pieces after him. Christians were always there for him. There was nothing dramatic, and no profound moments of revelation. Just a slow (even imperceptible) softening and warming. This culminated in him stopping by one evening with his girlfriend and her bags saying, "We both became Christians today! Obviously we can't live together 'til we get married so we were wondering if it's okay if she moves in with you for now?"

Then there is Roxanne from South America, who was new in town and just happened to bump into a Christian who brought her along to a meal she was having with the rest of us. Roxanne had had a formal Catholic upbringing but had never witnessed a group of people who took the gospel seriously or who loved Jesus so deeply. She came to a church meeting the next Sunday and although she didn't really understand a word the preacher said, she was impacted by his passion and intensity. She felt she had no option but to keep hanging out with these Christians, which she did in ordinary contexts like shopping, cleaning, drinking coffee, and walking. Again, there were no bright lights or sharp moments of clarity. But there was a steady thawing of a hard heart. She grew to understand grace through witnessing it in the lives of Christians who had become her friends.

I could tell you about Huw. He was really messed up when he just happened to sit next to a Christian at the bus stop. Broken marriage, no relationship with his kids, too much booze, too many drugs. He was intrigued by the book the guy was reading, and asked if he was one of those Christians who lived in the same projects he did. He eventually met the rest of them—ironically at the pub when he was drinking when he shouldn't have been. Huw's story is essentially the same as that of Josh and Roxanne, and countless others: real exposure to ordinary people living ordinary lives with clear gospel intentionality.

Mission isn't just about evangelism. It is just as much about discipleship. Seeing the gospel impact everyday details of our lives is nothing less than a miracle of grace. Seeing Christians share their possessions, homes, affections, ambitions, and time for the sake of the gospel is a phenomenon of the ordinary, of extraordinary proportions. Jake and Sarah have poured their lives into their neighbors. It's as messy and broken a situation as you could imagine. I so wish I could tell you that it had a happy ending and they've become Christians. But they haven't. In fact, they seem to have hardened their hearts and run harder after sin. But that's everyday mission. But gospel fruit is still growing in the mundane soil of ordinary life—if not their neighbors, at least gloriously in the hearts of Jake and Sarah.

Don't be impatient with the ordinary. Don't be seduced by a lust for the spectacular. Of course God can do remarkable things in remarkable ways. But most of the time He works in the ordinary and the mundane. Most of the time He uses ordinary people living very ordinary lives to spread the fame of His far-from-ordinary Son. As a very ordinary man I rejoice at this. And I resolve with grace to live my ordinary life extraordinarily well to the praise and fame of the Saviour.

STEVE TIMMIS is Global Director for the Acts29 Church Planting Network. He is an author, cofounder of The Crowded House, a church-planting initiative in Sheffield, UK, and Director of the Porterbrook Network, a training resource for mission. acts29europe.com

WHERE DOES EVERYDAY MISSION HAPPEN?

A couple of centuries after the Bible was completed, the North African bishop Augustine wrote a huge book called *The City of God*. In addition to defending Christianity against false charges of burning down the city of Rome, Augustine reintroduced the biblical idea we see this week, that Christians are called to live "as a city within a city." He calls Christians "the city of God," who actively involve ourselves in, and seek the redemption of, the "city of man" (as Augustine called it).

Where does everyday mission happen? In the city of man—which is filled with the natural places we each work, play, and live.[1] The idea of being a city within a city lays the dual foundation for this week: everyday mission happens as we live out our God-given identity, pursue His mission, and demonstrate the gospel, in the midst of—and for the good of—our mission fields.

DAY 21

MISSION IN A BAR?

THE SOUND OF (PINT) GLASS SHATTERING

ANSWER
Everyday mission happens in the darkness

READ
1 Corinthians 9:19–27

Mark followed our seminary's alcohol policy: abstinence "except for liturgical, ceremonial, medicinal, or other exceptional instances"[2] (which another friend once redefined tongue-in-cheek as "communion, anniversaries, and Thursday nights"). Mark got to know one not-yet-believing neighbor who, in mockery of the policy, always insisted they meet at a bar. They'd talk over Mark's soda and his friend's beer. The week after graduation, Mark ordered a craft brew. After some barside banter, his friend finally shook his head, "I'm not sure why, but I feel like I can really talk to you for the first time." A three-year barrier broke; the proverbial glass shattered. In the coming weeks, the friendship and discussion deepened.

"Where does everyday mission happen?" We start answering this week's question with a few others: "Where do people hang out?" "Where do our coworkers spend their time?" "Where do our neighbors congregate?" Wherever *that* is, that's where God sends us to carry out His mission.

LIGHT TO DARKNESS; NOT DARKNESS TO LIGHT

Consider Jesus' familiar words: "You are the light of the world. A city set on a hill cannot be hidden. Nor do people light a lamp and put it under a basket, but on a stand, and it gives light to all in the house. In the same way, let your light shine before others, so that they may see your good works and give glory to your Father who is in heaven."[3] Living out our faith in an unbelieving world is one way that God draws people to glorify Him. Conversely then, if we do *not* live out our faith in the darkness, we remove one way people can glorify God.

Charlotte woke up at four a.m. last night. When the babysitters had put her to bed, they hadn't flipped on her "night-night light." A train horn in the blackness startled her to tears. When I plugged in the tiny bulb, soft yellow light engulfed the room. The darkness was gone and she cuddled back to sleep. One of the most impacting facts I've ever learned is that physical light always goes into darkness; scientifically, darkness never comes to light. Darkness cannot overcome a candle; it must wait for the flame to flicker out. But when you flip a light switch, beams instantly fill the blackness. If we may spiritualize the image a bit, light goes into—and pushes back—darkness.

SURRENDERING THE TURF WAR

While going into the darkness can be scary, Jesus pushes us out of our baskets of easier mission—like inviting people to church gatherings or evangelistic events—to become lampstands on others' turf. To consider others' needs and comfort more highly than our own, we give up home field advantage. Sheffield, UK pastors Tim Chester and Steve Timmis list questions in their book *Total Church* to help us think like missionaries. "We sometimes ask people to imagine they are part of a church-planting team in a cross-cultural situation in some other part of the world:

→ What criteria would you use to decide where to live?

→ How would you approach secular employment?

→ What standard of living would you expect as pioneer missionaries?

→ What would you spend your time doing?

→ What opportunities would you be looking for?

→ What would your prayers be like?

→ What would you be trying to do with your new friends?

→ What kind of team would you want around you?

We find it easier to be radical in our thinking when we transplant ourselves outside our current situation. But we are as much missionaries here and now as we would be if were part of a cross-cultural team in another part of the world . . . These are the kinds of questions we should be asking wherever we are."[4] If you merely glanced at the questions, go back and actually answer them while thinking about another nation. Then answer again, this time objectively considering your current city. Are your second answers different than your current lifestyle? Convicting, isn't it?

DIFFERENT SHAPES OF THE SAME DARKNESS

Many followers of Jesus have what we'll call a "low indecency tolerance": if anything looks like it might, potentially, one day, maybe be sinful, we avoid it. Of course there's some wisdom in that: it's right to approach anything that incites our sin with wisdom, accountability, and close community. And we're by no means saying that true mission always includes going to a bar. But alcohol is an easy example of a broader idea: anything God doesn't label sin, He can use for His mission. The Bible acknowledges enjoyment of alcohol almost as much as it prohibits drunkenness.[5] As Mark learned, it can break down walls and deepen conversation. Could alcohol and other indiscretions help expand the gospel? If a neighbor hosts Friday night poker, a card table and $5 buy-in can be a venue for relationships. A few puffs on a cigar may be worth the opportunity to smoke and converse for a few hours. And so on.

A LONG LINE OF LEAVING OUR COMFORT ZONE

We're 130 percent certain that hairs are bristling on the back of some reader's neck right now. But before you spin off a blog post about our heresy, consider a couple other ways God sent people out of their comfort zones for His mission. These may seem normal after two thousand years of hindsight, but each was far more controversial in its day, than crisp cigars and aged bourbon are today.

The apostle Peter grew up believing anyone outside his own race was an outsider and that certain foods were taboo. But in a trio of rooftop visions, God redeems Peter's legalism: "Do not call anything impure that God has made clean."[6] God didn't just expand Peter's palate; He destroyed racial tension, and for the first time, God's mission extended to non-Jews: "Truly I understand that God shows no partiality, but in every nation anyone who fears him and does what is right is acceptable to him."[7] Later, Peter and Barnabas got scared kosher when legalistic Jews arrived at a Gentile feast.[8] And Jesus' disciples were scolded for not fasting correctly, while Jesus Himself hung out with the "wrong people" in the eyes of religious leaders, and was rebuked for healing, driving out spirits, and feeding on the Sabbath.[9]

From Sabbath, circumcision, and bacon, to drinking, gambling, and music, history proves legalism as one of religion's darker sides. The Pharisees often get a bad rap, but their many rules stemmed from a place more familiar than we'd like to admit. Realizing their inability to fulfill the Law by their own power, they fought back by adding layers of man-made protection instead of trusting Jesus as its fulfillment. Seattle pastor Mark Driscoll explains, "They were highly committed to getting back to the Scriptures and their brand of hard-line old-time religion. They developed a litany of laws to separate themselves from others in an effort to maintain their purity and righteousness by living in their own isolated culture."[10] Can't we see ourselves doing the same?

In order to protect holiness, we build fences around God's standards, to keep us one step removed from a sin. Then we build fences around those fences, to keep us from crossing that line. Eventually, we disconnect from a world that lives by a different standard, in the name of protecting our own. (That's the same world, by the way, from which Jesus specifically asked His Father *not* to remove us, but sent us into.[11]) When this happens, light leaves the darkness, and mission devolves to inviting the darkness to come to the light. In reality, someone will always be uncomfortable in mission. Are we willing to be the uncomfortable ones, for the sake of those to whom God sends us?

WILLING TO BECOME ALL THINGS?

Some Christians in Paul's day tried to force meal restrictions and even circumcision on those to whom they were on mission. But the apostle took a different path, becoming "all things to all people, that by all means I might save some." First Corinthians 9 shows that Paul didn't always reject legalism. At times, he gave up freedoms and submitted for the sake of those with tighter rules. We can't swing the pendulum of selfless discomfort to one extreme and ignore the other. But as we follow Paul as he follows the example of Christ, we might say, "To those who hit the poker tables, I pick up a few chips in order to comfort them with truth when they lose a big pot. For those who are religious, I became religious, that I might save them from their self-righteousness. For those who get drunk every Saturday, I go to the frat parties—not to get drunk, but that I might bless and care for those who are. For those who add rules to God's grace, I follow the rules in order to free them from trying to earn their salvation." And so on. There are hundreds of places God sends us on everyday mission. Many are out of our comfort zone, in the proverbial darkness, and on someone else's turf. But whoever *they* are and whatever *their turf* is, that's where we go and make disciples.

101 WAYS TO DEMONSTRATE THE GOSPEL

65 Attend community events: Instead of creating your own celebrations, join what's already happening in your community. Even if you feel out of place, it's a great way to be involved.

66 Go to their home: Everyone loves "home field advantage." So when you get invited to your neighbor, coworker, or friend's home, grab a gift, honor your host, and be a good guest.

67 Find the middle ground: Eat out, get dessert or drinks, see a movie or play, and meet beforehand to talk, or play basketball or golf. This may be a more comfortable first step, for both you and them.

HOME FIELD ADVANTAGE

DAY 22

DON'T MAKE CHURCH EVENTS YOUR ONLY EVANGELISM TOOL.

A pastor friend found out that his not-yet-believing neighbors were getting married. They already lived together and had a kid together. But they were taking the plunge. When my friend discovered this, he saw an open door for gospel conversation—finally! He congratulated them, reminded them that he was a pastor, and invited them to do premarital counseling with him. Offended, they rejected him outright. But a few days later his wife went over, also congratulated them, and simply asked if they were nervous about anything. As it turns out, they were: they were worried about changing their relationship; they were nervous about falling into patterns of their own parents. The pastor's wife told them she'd had the same fears and had even slipped into some poor habits in their decade of marriage, and asked if they wanted to come for dinner and talk about marriage. The first "yes" led to many late nights of food, laughter, and deep—even faith-focused—conversations.

Both the pastor and his wife wanted to start a relationship. Bob and I know that God can and does use whatever method He wants to bring people to Himself, even churchy things. But

ANSWER
Everyday mission happens in our own homes

READ
1 Peter 4:9–10

most of the people in our lives who don't know Jesus are often suspicious of—if not offended by—our attempts to invite them to religious events, be they Sunday gatherings, midweek Bible studies, religious counseling or classes, or church-sponsored activities.

What's the answer? The pastor's wife didn't invite the couple to anything programmed or "churchy"; she simply invited them into her life. Yesterday we encouraged giving up home field advantage and leaving our comfort zone for the sake of mission. Today we see that everyday mission can certainly occur in our homes. But it also asks us to consider how we invite people onto our turf: the way we treat them might make or break mission. Inviting people into our lives is harder than inviting people to church or an event. It takes vulnerability, generosity, and hospitality.

REAL LIFE = MESSY

Life is messy. In one episode of the sitcom *Everybody Loves Raymond*, Ray's parents get a new couch.[12] But they refuse to remove the plastic packing wrap from the couch, because they don't want it to get dirty. The discomfort and crunchy plastic hinder the couch from the one thing it's designed to do: be a comfortable place for a rear. We can keep people out of our lives for the same reason: our home is messy or our lives are messier. Either way we're embarrassed. Inviting someone in means we can't uphold the image of perfection they have of us—maybe even the image we want them to have. It's easier to keep people at an arm's length; to invite them to an event instead of dinner; to keep our lives pretty.

As missionaries, we sacrifice ourselves and invite people in: into our homes, our tables, our yards, our kids' toys, our pools, our hobbies, our free time, our cars. Unless you drive a windowless van. Then don't invite them into your car. Yes, it's awkward to invite someone over for the first time. Yes, a first dinner might involve silence if you don't know them well. Yes, someone might spill something. Yes, they might ask you something you can't answer. And yes, they might find something imperfect about you. Because you're imperfect like every other human.

In *A Meal with Jesus*, Tim Chester's fascinating look at mission and community around the table, he references the weight of inviting people in: "In a famous essay, anthropologist Mary Douglas showed that in all cultures meals represent 'boundary markers.' They mark the boundaries between different levels of intimacy and acceptance."[13] Giving a similar historical view of meals, scholar Scott Bartchy writes, "Being welcomed at a table for the purpose of eating food with another person had become a ceremony richly symbolic of friendship, intimacy and unity."[14] These images shed new perspective on Jesus' meals with tax collectors, sinners, Samaritans, and prostitutes, Peter's dream, and the banquet images of Jesus.[15] On one level, inviting folks in says, "You're in my home; I'm at your disposal," and, "You're in the inner circle." It's difficult to hide. On another level, it speaks to reconciliation and acceptance. Everyday mission happens on your turf as we reach an uncomfortable, "laying-down-your-life" level of vulnerability.

GENEROSITY LIKE JESUS

Ask restaurant servers why they hate working Sunday lunch: Christians are known to be stingy. But it's difficult to find a better way to display fruit of the gospel than sacrificial generosity: in Jesus' first miracle, He brought the best wine of the night. God's blessing on Abram was for the purpose of blessing others. In Christ, Christians have been "blessed . . . with every spiritual blessing."[16] Eugene Peterson summarizes God's call to love others "extravagant."[17] And on we could go. The generous outpouring of life on a cross took great sacrifice. But Jesus was willing to display the ultimate generosity for the sake of others and the "joy that was set before him."[18] As we sacrifice (far less than Jesus did); as we bless, serve, spend money and time on others (even extravagant money and time); as we bring the best food, drink, music, and "life," we display gospel generosity. If we invite people onto our turf, let's show them the time of their lives. We've been abundantly blessed, so let's abundantly bless. Caesar Kalinowski, among others, has exhorted, "Church, we should be the most celebratory people on the planet! We get to live forever! . . . People in your city should be going, 'I don't know if I believe what they believe, but whoa do they party.'"[19]

A SERVANT IN OUR OWN HOMES?

Today's principle is summed up in one word: "hospitality." Contrary to popular belief, biblical hospitality is not just Christians hanging out together. The Bible often calls that "fellowship."[20] It's not just making coffee for people on a Sunday morning. The Bible would more likely call that "making coffee for people." From God's command that Israel make space for the foreigner, sojourner, and outcast to His exhortation that Israel feed from its own crops; from the repeated call to love your neighbor "*as yourself*," to His parable of inviting the outcasts of society to a feast; from His own meals with tax collectors, sinners, and prostitutes, to even washing His disciples' feet, we see true, biblical hospitality:[21] God's people make strangers feel welcome. So yes, we can extend invitations to church

101 WAYS
TO DEMONSTRATE THE GOSPEL

68 Throw a party: Fire up the grill, grab the Slip 'n Slide for the kids, put on some classic rock, and spend extra time and money to serve the best food and drink you can afford. And provide beer or wine, even if you don't touch it.

69 Be open to surprise visits: Make it known that your door is always open, your TV always available, and extra dinner always made. Other than time reserved as family-only, use your home generously.

70 Have folks at your table often: Every meal doesn't have to be a big party or fancy feast; simply invite another friend or couple, eat the spaghetti you were planning on, and share it.

71 Make extra: The biblical concept of loving others promoted generosity. So whether dinner, brownies, garden crops, or whatever else, make more than needed and give it away, to whomever God leads you.

events at times, because faith is an important part of our lives. But more often, we extend invitations to a party, dinner, concert, or ball game. Hospitality happens as we invite them into our homes and our whole lives.

To be clear, hospitality doesn't exclude Christians. Paul was taken in when he was in danger, throughout the early Church Jesus' followers took care of those in need among themselves, and sometimes people just need a place to be welcomed, rest, or heal.[22] We all need a door to knock on in a two a.m. emergency. But just as much as Christian people need those things at times, so do those who don't know Jesus. Like evangelism, hospitality is a spiritual gift,[23] which means it comes more naturally to some people than others. But like mission, hospitality is also a command in the Scriptures, to *all* of God's people.

Everyday mission on our own turf means that rather than an honored host, our paradoxical posture in our own homes is one of a humble servant. I love that nearly every day, Charlotte asks us who's coming over for dinner. I'm not sure if it's good or bad that she's often disappointed the days we tell her it's just our family. Her toddler innocence embodies 1 Peter 4's encouragement: to an incredible level of selfless hospitality, and to steward that hospitality as a gift.[24] Do you serve others in and through your home? Is your table a place where strangers feel welcome? Can people feel the extravagant love of Jesus when they walk through your gate? Do you sacrifice the comfort, privacy, and prettiness of your home for God's mission? If so, your home is a venue for vulnerability, generosity, and hospitality, as you steward God's grace in your life for the sake of His mission.

DAY 23

ANSWER
Everyday mission happens where we incarnate ourselves

READ
John 1:14–18

A STAKE IN THE GROUND

"THE REASON WHY CHRISTIANS WERE SO EFFECTIVE IN EVANGELISM . . . WAS BECAUSE THEY WERE BOTH 'LIKE AND UNLIKE.'"

So says New York pastor and author Tim Keller. Clear as mud? Keller explains: "On the one hand, when New Yorkers . . . look at Christians, if we are utterly different than the other people of Manhattan—utterly different in our sensibility, and our cultural ways, and our interests, and everything—then they're gonna say, 'Christianity's not for me.' But also we have to be unlike other Manhattanites. We have to have such high integrity; we have to have a compassion for the poor that goes beyond just talking about it; we have to have poise in suffering; we have to be clearly, deeply involved in the lives of other Christians. [Because] non-Christians in Manhattan do not see strong community. They do not see people handling suffering well. They see people saying we need to help the poor but not actually doing it. They see a lot of people who, in order to get ahead in New York, do all sorts of shady practices without much integrity. We have to be 'like but unlike' New Yorkers. We have to have relational integrity. We have to have the courage to open our mouths . . . and an ability to have really great relationships."[25]

"Like and unlike" may be the most balanced way we've ever heard, to describe the concept of incarnational mission. Modeled after Jesus' own mission, incarnational mission is embedding ourselves deeply into our mission field, ministering in ways that fit its unique rhythm and needs, and staying there for the long haul. Think again about cross-cultural missions: while "missionaries" who pop into a nation for a week do beneficial work, it's the long-term missionaries who love, weep, and rejoice with those they're serving for years. But even the goal for many long-term missionaries is to raise up local leaders. Because they're within their own culture, indigenous leaders are like their mission field. Because they're *Christians* within their culture, they're also unlike it.

Jesus was a pinnacle of "like—unlike." He "became flesh" (like those He was sent to), and He is "the Word . . . the only Son from the Father . . ." (obviously not like us).[26] While Paul was a traveling missionary and a model for sending, Jesus was an incarnational missionary and a model for staying. For three decades, He lived and worked in the small village of Nazareth. For His entire public ministry, He stayed within seventy miles of His home. He did literally everything with people in a small mission field, for all one thousand-or-so days of His mission. Then He died in and for His mission field. Christians are an incarnational people, pursuing an incarnational Christ. But let's check our motives: incarnation isn't a new missions program; it's a lifestyle—one birthed out of love. As in any other realm of society, if we love someone we want to be with them.

DWELLING IN OUR MISSION FIELDS

What does it look like to incarnate ourselves into our everyday mission fields? We've already discussed learning your location and joining its hyper-local rhythms (see Day 12), but let us suggest a few proactive ways you can commit to the unique area God has sent you to.

Eat, Drink, and Shop There

When I discovered Thai food, I fell in culinary love. The herbs, the spicy sweet, the complexity . . . It's probably what we'll eat at the Marriage Supper of the Lamb. But Jess and I don't have Thai food near my house. In fact, the two best places for curry in Fort Worth are both fifteen minutes away. In Fort Worth language, that might as well put them in Dallas. I pass through four distinct parts of town to get to one; five to the other. Within walking distance from my house, though, is a string of tasty local restaurants. So I have a choice to make: do I make the half-hour round trip to fill my Thai Select or Happy Bowl fix, or do I invest time and money in my hyper-local businesses, see some neighbors, and build relationships we've started with Nahme or Peter, who own Chadra and Old Neighborhood Grill? The same applies to oil changes, haircuts, groceries, and most goods and services. That's the incarnational question: stay or go, for the stuff of everyday life? (Confession: I still sneak away for Thai once every couple of weeks or so. I'm a sinner in need of grace.)

Recreate There

Since I (Bob) had a hip replacement, doctors don't like me jogging. So I'm riding a bike. The guy who's helping me adjust to cycling wouldn't consider himself a Jesus follower. He began to work on my bike and found this wrong and that wrong. My wife got nervous about how much the fixes were going to cost. But it was mission. It wasn't cheap, but I value the friendship with the guy, and we talk frequently. He even wants me to join his biking club. I don't have to start my thing; I can be a part of his thing. Instead of starting "Christian stuff," let's just be Christians in their stuff. Incarnation leads us to recreate in our mission fields. Tyler and Bethany host a front-yard movie night and invite neighbors. Several ladies we know take their kids to the zoo together and invite neighbors and friends to come along. Don't join the cheapest gym if it's across town; join the one you can walk or bike to. Play in the park instead of your backyard. Walk your neighborhood instead of a track.

Work There

Working in your mission field can look a few different ways, and we acknowledge it can't apply to everyone. But it *can* apply to more people than you'd think. You may just have to be creative. In addition to seeing work as a mission field, a second form of incarnation is to work from home, or from a local coffee shop or pub. Mobile workplaces are increasingly common. Even if just a half day each week, some of us can carve out space for relationships with others in our mission field. Obviously you're paid to get work done, so we're not suggesting you simply lounge around and talk to folks. On Day 6, we said that mission at work largely exists "in the cracks." That's true no matter where that work happens. But the two-minute conversations with the person at the next table; taking five minutes to help your neighbor move furniture; and the regularity of seeing the same barista, can all lay the foundation for deeper mission. We also believe one way God calls some people to work in their mission field is to actually change jobs in order to be there. This may seem extreme, but Jesus was known for calling His people to extreme sacrifice for His sake and for the gospel.[27] Matt took a pay cut to travel less and keep evenings free. Luke turned down a job in order to stay in Fort Worth. Bethany took a new job, closer to her mission field. Extreme? Yes. Illogical? Likely. But worth it? Absolutely.

Live There

Can't work in your current mission field? Can't quit your job? But because of your commute, don't have time to meet folks where you live? Consider an opposite extreme: if you can't work where you live, God might send you to live where you work. Whether you move for your job or another reason, the final incarnational practice is to go live among those you're on mission to. As Alan Hirsch puts it, "Incarnational mission implies a *real and abiding* incarnational presence among a group of people. Quite simply, it means that if you want to reach the local *gangstas*, you are going to have to live where they live and hang out where they hang out. Or it might mean that if you want to plant a church in a given suburb, you should really think about living there. Why? Because you cannot become part of the organic life of a given community if you are not present to it and do not experience its cultural rhythms, its life, and its geography."[28]

RETURNING TO "LIKE AND UNLIKE"

Eat, drink, shop, recreate, work, and live. Each of these—and likely other everyday things in your unique situations—puts us among and with those to whom God sent us. In these ways we live like the field God sent us to. But we do so with integrity, displaying generosity, treating people with grace and respect, living a life with different motives, and (to preview next week's topic) talking openly but not forcefully about our faith. In these ways we are gloriously, sacrificially *unlike* our mission field. Over time, as we choose to stay instead of go, we have more opportunities, build more relationships, create a stronger foundation, and see more doors open to demonstrate the gospel. That's a picture of incarnational mission.

101 WAYS TO DEMONSTRATE THE GOSPEL

72 Make a local watering hole "yours": It was a coffee shop in *Friends*; a bar in *Cheers*. Go to a place often, and get to know the workers and regulars. Have meetings, and even have a Bible study there.

73 Work out with others: Gyms can be hubs of community. Join with others; talk between exercises; take a class; bless the staff. As a secondary benefit, you might live a bit longer.

74 Buy local: You generally get to know workers at "non-chain" stores and restaurants better than at corporately run ones. And you bless your city by supporting local business in your mission field.

75 Learn a second language: Learning a language that isn't primary in your context shows great honor, care, and intentionality, and enhances your ability to connect meaningfully with others.

FULL HOUSE

"THIS COULD BLOW UP IN OUR FACES."

On our Serve Sundays, the whole City Church family serves—including kids. Early on, we wondered if we'd only be able to simulate serving: create a fake patch of dirt for them to "plant flowers" in to distract them while the grown-ups did the real work. One of our first sites involved building an outdoor classroom for a local school. We thought kids + outside + busy parents = recipe for disaster. We thought it might blow up. But it was amazing. From much younger than we thought, kids got involved. They picked up branches. They planted flowers. They got supplies. They painted. Yes, we painted after them. And yes, a few had to be deep-cleaned afterward. But there was such benefit that most sites since that day equip kids to actually serve others.[29] We pray for the kids, and pray with kids for the people we serve. We remind them that we bless because Jesus first blessed us. There's no way they all "get it," but some do. Even our youngest get to participate in reconciling brokenness—not just with their heads or hearts, but with their paint-covered little hands.

A DIFFERENT MARK OF SUCCESS

This rings true not just for serving others, but for other elements of our everyday mission. A world map hangs in my home office, next to a

ANSWER
Everyday mission happens where our family is involved

READ
Matthew 18:1–6

window that looks out over our neighbors' homes. Many nights as I put Charlotte to bed, we go into my office and look out the window to pray for our neighbors, or talk about and pray for whatever place on the map she points to. After a few months, Charlotte now prays more often than I do: "Dear-God-thank-you-for-our-neighbors-please-save-their-souls-amen." Just as when she prays that God will save her own soul amen, I doubt she understands what she's saying. But she *does* understand, on some level, that we care about others. She grasps that we pause to consider them. She gets to see pictures of, and hear about, parts of the world different than hers. And she even remembers them. (At least, when she points at Australia, she consistently giggles, "G'day mate"—apologies, Alan Hirsch.)

The key for bringing families into mission is setting different expectations for different family members. "Success" will not look the same for a forty-year-old, a thirteen-year-old, and a two-year-old. Maybe success for the two-year-old is engaging long enough to do something for someone else, while for the teen it's their ability to explain the gospel motivation for mission. (Or maybe success for the teen is also engaging long enough to do something for someone else?) But we do not disallow children's participation just because they can't do as well or grasp as much as older family members.

LESSONS FROM OUR CHILDREN . . . ABOUT OUR CHILDREN

Many opportunities to involve children in mission aren't difficult, but they ask families to reorient themselves for the sake of that mission. We don't think it's a stretch to say that family and children are common idols today. This has likely been true throughout history, since one of Jesus' consistent drumbeats was putting Himself above His followers' families.[30] Even well-meaning Christians find it difficult to bring our families into mission because we over-value and over-protect our children.

Ironically, in today's verses Jesus uses children themselves, to teach us a lesson about children on mission. What can a baby do? Nothing. Young children are completely reliant on something outside of themselves: to provide for, care for, nourish, teach them, and do everything for them. Elementary kids have figured out how to walk and feed themselves, but they're full of questions. The rebellious teen needs Mom and Dad more than they let on. And if the relationship is healthy, even adults ask for parental advice. "Receiving the kingdom . . . like a little child" speaks of our great inability before God, in all of life. It calls parents to reject our ability, self-reliance, and our own work and action, to produce anything godly or good. "Faith like a child" admits that we need something outside ourselves, and greater than ourselves. The only right position to take before our heavenly Father is "humble . . . like a child." We are full of nothing but a desperate need for God the Spirit to work in every aspect of our lives.

We often confess that type of faith—or at least desire it—in many areas of life. But today we zoom in on an ironic area many have a hard time trusting God with: our children. Without God, we are as powerless in raising children as we are in any other aspect of life. We lack the ability to ensure their comfort, safety, success, and salvation. Yet instead of trusting God "like a child" *for our child*, we put hope in our ability as parents, in the best schools money can buy, in church programs, and in Christian organizations. In these we trust, to keep kids from scraped knees, to propel them into the highest-earning career, and to guard against sin. We may not see it until our kids are eighteen or twenty-one, but even these seemingly good things can fail to deliver.[31] Like every false god does.

Certainly it's good to want what's best for our child. Jesus even affirms this: "Which one of you, if his son asks him for bread, will give him a stone?"[32] But today's reading ends with a caution against misunderstanding Matthew 18 and similar verses. Many parents read Jesus' exhortation to keep children from sin, lock their kiddos in a proverbial Christian tower, and throw the key into the moat to guard them from the dragon and its fire-breathing temptation out there. But could it be that our attempts to protect our children from sin might actually prompt them *to* sin? By taking them out of the world, we disallow their obedience to God's command to go into it.

Even your kid is called to God's mission Let us draw a fine line as we battle our idols *of* children and pursue mission *with* children:

→ It's not a sin to want our kids to do well in life, but it might be sinful to prioritize their educational institution over God's call to engage mission.

→ It's good to protect your children, but it's disobedient to God to hide them away from the world God sends us into.

→ It's right to shape your child's worldview, but it's dangerous to keep them from hearing any other: Bob and I both see children in college deny the faith parents instilled for decades, because they've never heard opposition before.

→ It's not even wrong to want to be efficient, but if in the name of efficiency we deny kids' opportunities to join our mission at times, we might miss out on chances to "train up a child in the way he should go"; to "bring them up in the discipline and instruction of the Lord" regarding the mission of God.[33]

101 WAYS TO DEMONSTRATE THE GOSPEL

75 Double (or triple) date: Be intentional about dates and share some with other couples. Especially if you have children, a grown-ups only evening provides the deepest conversation you'll ever have!

76 Consider public school: Often seen as less desirable than alternatives, most of your neighbors attend and share an interest in that school; the door's wide open, the door for great, local relationships.

77 Join a PTA or become a room parent: Bless teachers, administration, kids, and other parents by providing treats, parties, and organization for the school. Plus it's a non-forced way to meet neighbors.

78 Coach your kids and their friends: In sports, music, or whatever, encourage kids, battle their idols, meet parents and other coaches, and display a gospel-infused view of competition and fun.

JOINING YOUR CHILD'S MISSION

We've already seen that parents are the primary disciplers of our children. Family is a mission field God sends us to. But if they're redeemed, family members are also on mission with us. Part of raising our children well is helping them participate in God's mission. If they're not yet redeemed, parents expose our children to the world around while they still trust us most. And as kids form friendships with other kids, parents can build relationships with parents. So rather than signing our children up for a Christian little league, put them on a city team. Instead of a church-based preschool or high school, enroll them in classes at the local museum, zoo, or arts academy. Send them to the school where everyone else on your block does. As a parent, be involved: pray with your kids for their team and classmates. Pray for their teachers, coaches, and parents. Join your child in their mission field: serve on the PTA, volunteer in their classroom, coach that Little League team. And as with every other resource God's entrusted to us, we steward our family and even children well, as opportunities God gives both us and our kids to engage His mission.

DAY 25

JESUS' BEAUTIFUL, BROKEN BRIDE

IT SENT SHOCK WAVES THROUGOUT CAMPUS.

ANSWER
Everyday mission happens in our church families

READ
Matthew
7:15–27

As you might imagine, seminaries are full of Jesus-y people, from suit-clad conservatives to library-dwelling linguists to edgy liberals who buck the system by (prepare for a shock) wearing flip-flops to class. Our grad school was filled with religion majors, pastors and interns, and private school teachers. Everyone was religious; most were active in some form of church; many spent spring breaks and summers in overseas missions or student ministry camps. So imagine the bombshell when a student realized he'd never actually known Jesus. Students and professors alike were stunned, then celebratory at the revelation. The student was a son of a prominent pastor, a rising star in the student ministry world, and someone who knew—and could teach—the Bible better than most of his peers. Apparently it happens more than you might expect: God redeems people who are already in seminary, or working at churches. And praise Him that He does!

The initial shock is understandable: we can easily assume that because someone is part of a Christian school, group, and church, they must be redeemed. But as today's verses point out, their religion may be misleading. Whether we attend a seminary or Christian school, are involved with a Christian organization, or are simply part of a local church family, we regularly find ourselves in some of the most forgotten places everyday mission happens: within "Christian" circles. Today we consider two elements of mission inside the Church: seeing it as an mission field and getting other Christians to join us on mission.

FRUIT AND FOUNDATION: MARKS OF FAITH

Today is not a license to look under every rock for false prophets and fake Christians. Only God can know the condition of souls for sure, so we approach today with great humility and much prayer. But it should spark awareness: how many in our own circles look and act redeemed, but are potentially deceived? As we pursue everyday mission in Christian circles, today's verses offer two concurrent marks of redemption: the fruit in our lives and the foundation of our hearts.

When rightly rooted, our lives flourish with good fruit. In Luke 3, John the Baptist rebukes many who come to be baptized merely to escape hell. To put it in a common term today, John calls those who view Jesus as mere "fire insurance"—whose so-called salvation makes no impact on daily life—a "brood of vipers."[34] His charge is that those who are truly redeemed will bear fruit. The following verses are examples of this fruit: those who were selfish become generous; those who stole become honest (and in Zacchaeus's case in Luke 19, display the gospel by reconciling the brokenness they caused); those who trusted their own ability turn to God for provision. Galatians 5 explains the difference between fruit of the flesh and fruit of the Spirit. Romans 5–7 give marks of the "old man" versus the "new man." Seen throughout the Bible, redemption leads to fruit.

On the other end of the spectrum, good works—which look like spiritual fruit—can stem from misguided motives. An early song from musical duo Shane and Shane encapsulate well the mystery of working hard but lacking depth: "Your child is busy with the work of God and taking him for granted / Got a lot to do today; kingdom work's the game I play / Lord my serving You replaced me knowing You."[35] Religious acts, having the right answers, doing the proper things, and even looking repentant or wise can give the impression that we must be children of God. Those Jesus speaks of in Matthew 7 preached, did great works, and even performed miracles *in His name.* Yet He still never knew them. Anything but Jesus is a failing foundation of faith. Winds of truth expose our misplaced footholds, and "great [is] the fall" of even our greatest attempts. Good fruit is only good if its roots are in the right foundation.

PURSUING NOT-YET-BELIEVERS IN OUR CHURCHES

Due to theological misunderstanding or even misinformation about salvation, mission in our churches can be tricky. Claiming that someone might not be a Christian is a bold claim, and can cause ripples. But if people in our churches and Christian circles lack fruit, we have to lovingly pursue them: it's our responsibility as brothers and sisters who love them more than their opinion of us. Even if they are believers, they need discipleship in areas where disbelief or idols pull them from obeying God. If they are not redeemed, they need loving relationships and intentional discipleship even more. Either way, the gospel needs to redeem at least some area of their life.

Do they exhibit patterns of sinful or unwise behavior? Do they put other authorities over the authority of God? Do they seem unrepentant or uncaring toward their sin? Do they lack the desire to grow in spiritual concepts and practices? Matthew outlines a process to address such questions.[36] While this passage is often labeled "Church Discipline," "discipline" has the same root as "disciple": the goal of loving confrontation, humble rebuke, and gentle questions is stated throughout this passage: that the brokenness in our brother would be restored, to God and community. And while the final step of this process is often interpreted, "cut them out of your life," we see in Jesus a far different view of "Gentile[s] and tax collector[s]." He didn't throw them away; He pursued them, loved them, demonstrated the gospel to them, and sought their redemption. In other words, this process encourages us to act the same toward sinners in our churches, as sinners outside our churches.

GETTING YOUR CHURCH TO JOIN YOU IN MISSION

We must close today with another question that begs to be answered about everyday mission and God's Church: "How can I get my church to join me on mission?" A danger of realizing God's call to mission in your city is that we can easily become frustrated—even haughty—toward those who have not yet realized the same call. This has led to exasperation within churches and anger toward church leadership. Let us suggest five ways to help direct your church to mission, especially if you're not in charge of its direction.

Model Mission

Hopefully you've seen this by now, but everyday mission is not a church program. It's a lifestyle, birthed from the new identity God gives us in the gospel. If books and teachings like ours stir something in you, don't despise your church if is not yet stirred. But don't wait for your church to tell you to "go make disciples"; Jesus already has. Start practicing mission, share stories of God's work in the lives of you and others, remain humble before those who don't yet understand, and lead by example in the calling God placed on each of His people.

Invite Others to Learn with You

We know of this great little *Field Guide* you can walk others through . . . But seriously, we can more easily wrap our minds around God's mission and its implications for our lives when we can discuss and practice with others. Form a study group around missional theory and theology, or a "mission lab" to regularly and corporately put that theory into practice.

Involve Those Who Oppose You

Since you're living out biblical commands, you have nothing to hide. Rather than keep your study group or mission lab private, invite those who understand it least, or who oppose you most. You build bridges, humble yourself, and maybe learn with them. Even if they say "no," you've kept your integrity and tried to include them.

Respect Your Leaders

Follow a biblical encouragement: submit to your church's leaders—even to be a joy to them.[37] A common fear in many churches—especially among leaders—is secret subversion. We can both speak from pastoral experience: when someone forms meetings of people within a church without telling anyone in leadership, yellow flags go up. After all, we are charged with guarding our flocks. On behalf of our pastoral peers, may we humbly ask you to explain to leaders what you're doing and why? And to affirm them instead of comparing your newfound love for mission to their inadequately in leading the same?

Don't Leave

The Church is Jesus' bride—it's the family of God. On one hand, if everyone who pursues mission leaves their churches, those churches never grow in this area of weak-

101 WAYS
TO DEMONSTRATE THE GOSPEL

79 Admit your own need: Before you can call others out in their sin, invite them to speak into yours. It exhibits humility, and earns more of a right in their eyes when you speak into theirs.

80 Do "church discipline" often: The first step—addressing one another's sin—should be far less a heavy-handed formality and much more a function of everyday discipleship, in loving community.

81 Share missional stories with leaders: Even if leaders don't get it, your mission should benefit the church—new believers lead to new members. Celebrate the doors God opens and fruit He bears.

82 Involve not-yet-believers in the church: It won't likely be your first step, but it should be a step, down the line: involve them in your life, community, and at some point, events and gatherings within your church.

ness. On the other hand, mission without a love for a church introduces not-yet-believers to Jesus while neglecting His bride. There are exceptions: the time sometimes arrives for some to leave. If that's true, leave well—with honor, humility, and respect. But more often, stay—for the sake of Jesus, His bride, its mission, and those He redeems.

As much as we acknowledge their beautiful brokenness, we believe in local churches, their biblical leadership, their place in God's mission, and unity amongst their members. Churches are full of sinners who need to be redeemed, and sinning saints who already have been. Just like you and us. We cannot plead this point enough: let us be wise, humble, and prayerful, both as we pursue God's mission toward those in our churches, and as we pursue mission together *alongside* others in them.

"WHERE" QUESTIONS FOR YOU TO WORK THROUGH

☐ **GENERAL:** What impacted you the most this week? What was new, convicting, or confusing? What was difficult? What do you need to discuss with others?

☐ **GENERAL:** Where's your heart, as you consider God's mission? What are you currently thinking? What's motivating you? What scares you? How is God moving in you?

☐ **DAY 21:** What are some things you find yourself labeling as "wrong," that the Bible doesn't define as sin or even inherently unwise? Why do you call them "wrong"?

☐ **DAY 21:** What are some specific ways you'd be willing to stretch—or leave—your comfort zone for the sake of going onto their turf (whoever "their" is for you)?

☐ **DAY 22:** Are you more comfortable inviting not-yet-believers to church gatherings, Bible studies, church events, a common ground space (restaurant, etc.), or into your home? Why?

☐ **DAY 22:** What are some specific ways you can be vulnerable, generous, hospitable, and servant-like with your own home? Why will it be difficult to do so? In what ways can God and others push you to use your home for the sake of His mission?

☐ **DAY 23:** In what practical ways are you "like" your mission field? In what ways are you "unlike" them? How does a biblical balance of "like and unlike" help your mission?

☐ **DAY 23:** Look at the suggested ways to incarnate yourself into your mission field. Do you eat, drink, and shop there? Do you recreate there? Do you work there? Do you live there? If not, why? Where specifically might God be leading you to incarnate yourself more?

☐ **DAY 24:** In what ways do you idolize your family or children? How does that play out in everyday life? How does that hinder both your mission and theirs?

☐ **DAY 24:** What are practical ways your children can join you on mission? What are practical ways you can join your children on theirs?

☐ **DAY 25:** Why are both fruit and foundation necessary in the lives of true believers? Considering ways this book encourages you to view and approach not-yet-believers, how might you approach those in your church, whose fruit and foundation you question, in humble, loving ways?

☐ **DAY 25:** If it hasn't happened yet, how can you specifically pray for your church family to realize God's call to everyday mission? From our suggestions or otherwise, in what practical ways can you humbly help guide your church to join you in pursuing that call? Who needs to be informed?

☐ **GENERAL:** Look back over this week's "Everyday Mission Ideas." What additional, practical things can you come up with, specific to your personality, gifting, and mission field, to live out God's mission? Share your ideas online with the hashtag #everydaymission.

MY MISSION
MARY DEMUTH

LE ROURET, FRANCE [38]

I approach this subject from a familial perspective, with children ages sixteen, thirteen, and ten. As one who espouses that the first true, genuine, infectious community is the family,

I believe that how we demonstrate Jesus to our families in the midst of our culture's shift will have deep and lasting impact not only on our culture but also on the kingdom of God.

Our family spent two and a half years living in post-Christian France—all this during our children's formative years. Through many tears and hard-won discussions, we learned to thrive. We developed what we now call Conversational Parenting, where we parented around the dinner table.

We try to have the kinds of conversations that make our kids wildly enthusiastic about our home. We've created the kind of community that's haven-like—a place where kids aren't afraid to be themselves, where they're applauded for being comfortable in their own skin. This is not at the expense of engagement, nor is it embracing protectionism. It's this kind of authentic interaction that not only benefits children and families, but if taken to its logical conclusion, helps everyone in our communities of faith better interact with the world around us. Havens do that.

So, in the land of postmodernism on steroids, we saw our children experience redemption.

→ Our eldest daughter led her friend to Jesus after loving her, talking to her, and praying for her over a year.

→ Our son voiced frustration to his friend's parents (in French) when they showed a demonic film for a birthday party.

→ Our youngest daughter met Jesus in France. Her father baptized her in the Mediterranean Sea.

Bishop Whipple, known as the "apostle to the Indians," said this: "For the last thirty years, I have looked for the face of Christ in the people with whom I have disagreed." His words clearly expose the paradox and beauty of what I call engagement and purity. James 1:27 illustrates: "Religion that God our Father accepts as pure and faultless is this: to look after orphans and widows in their distress [engagement] and to keep oneself from being polluted by the world [purity]."

Abram understood this countercultural relationship between pursuing God and engaging people. In Genesis 12:8, it says, "From there...he pitched his tent, with Bethel on the west and Ai on the east." Oswald Chambers expands this in saying, "Bethel is the symbol of communion with God; Ai is the symbol of the world. Abram pitched his tent between the two."

In a hyper-shifting culture, our tendency is to polarize to extremes—to run toward purity at the expense of engaging culture, or to embrace culture at the expense of a vibrant, connected faith. The pathway to the kind of faith that seeks to find Jesus on the face of those who disagree is based solidly on the irresistibility of Jesus Christ. He is our example of engaging the culture, yet staying pure. He had dirty hands and a clean heart—something I hope to emulate.

As we value Jesus as the central part of our communities, whether that be our family as a microcosm of biblical community, or our churches and small groups, we will begin to see a winsome transition in the culture around us—an opening to the paradoxical ways of the kingdom.

MARY DEMUTH is an author, speaker, wife, and mom. The author of several fiction and nonfiction books, Mary mentors writers and loves to write and speak about the redemptive hand of God in impossible situations. marydemuth.com

HOW DO I SHARE THE GOSPEL WITH-OUT KILLING THE RELATIONSHIP?

"HELLO, MY NAME IS _____" So say stick-on name tags at corporate events, PTA meetings, neighborhood mixers, and school parties. Ever watched people's reactions to the name tags? Some glance at it for a split second when they think you're not looking, so you think they remember you from last year's holiday party. Others will look long and hard, even making up pneumonic devices to remember your name. Out loud. Two feet in front of you. But regardless of the response, the name tag exists to break down barriers and enable conversation.

This final week answers the question, "HOW do I share the gospel?" More so, "How do I do so without killing the relationship?" This piece of the missional conversation must not be ignored. Actions are great; service helps; our lifestyle opens doors. Everything we've said so far can help pave the way for the gospel to be explicitly shared. But we can't stop at the end of Week Five. Because mission that never explicitly points to Jesus is not true mission. The gospel is the good news; it's the Word of life. Whether written or spoken, "good news" and "words" must always be proclaimed. But we don't seem to know how. Many Christians display the fruit of the gospel, but the moment we're asked about it, we clam up. When doors open to sharing the gospel, it seems we'd rather ease it back shut than burst through it. Let us help you: sharing the gospel isn't as hard as many of us think it is. In fact, the gospel can even be integrated into everyday conversation, in ways that won't get us shoved out of a car or have water thrown in our faces. And no, we're not telling you that the first way to share the gospel is to constantly wear a "Hello, my name is ____" name tag.

DAY 26

BAIT AND SWITCH?

TEXAS HAS ONLY THREE SEASONS PER YEAR.

Unlike most of the nation's spring, summer, fall, and winter, we have springtime, ridiculously hot, and football season. From preseason to Super Bowl Sunday, football talk is everywhere. From fantasy teams, to social media feeds; from pro and college jerseys worn proudly in the grocery, to conversations and watch parties, our world revolves around our teams. You may not love football, but something is just as important to you as football is to the stereotypical fan. The next installment in your favorite movie trilogy, your family, your job, your church, a new restaurant you visited, a big project you're working on; whatever it is, we all talk about what's important to us.

AVOIDING JESUS

If you're a Christian, it's likely you'd consider Jesus more important to you than football. Although sometimes we wonder about some men in our churches . . . And yet, this Cornerstone of our very lives, motives, actions, and decisions often becomes the least-discussed aspect of our entire lives. Many Christians pull a "bait and switch" on those around us. You know that image: a newspaper ad lures you to a store, where you find out there were "only ten at the special price, but look what else we have . . ." If we've

ANSWER
We share the gospel by being open from day one

READ
Romans 1:16–17

gotten to know a neighbor for nine months, and only then we reveal that we follow Jesus, we've done the same thing; they question our motives, wonder about our relationship, and feel like we've lied to them. And we have; as the courtroom oath goes, we've showed and told "the truth," but not "the whole truth so help me God." How do we share the gospel without killing the relationship? The first way is to be open about our faith from day one.

We commonly avoid discussing faith for one of three reasons. First, it's divisive. Second, we're nervous: "What if they then ask us a question we can't answer?" Third, since they don't follow Jesus, we lack the shared experience that a football game easily provides, so we wonder if we have any common ground. But each of these reasons breaks down. First, if we incarnate ourselves into a mission field, eventually people know we follow Jesus. Our neighbors see us pull out of our driveways every Sunday, frantic and late, or see Bible-toting friends enter our home every Wednesday. Second, when (not if) they ask a question we can't answer, we have two viable options. We can answer from our own experience, since that is initially more meaningful than cold, hard facts. Or we can show humility: "I haven't studied that specific element of faith yet, so I don't know." Then we can go find the answer and honor them by remembering to follow up. Third, we may lack the shared experience of faith, but we're normal humans, so we likely have plenty to talk about.

A PERCEPTION OF SHAME

One thing comes across in our lack of sharing the gospel: shame. If we can't look someone in the eye and talk about our personal experience with Jesus with confidence, we appear to be ashamed of the very thing we claim as most important to us. We go directly against today's exhortation to Roman Christians, *not* to be ashamed of the gospel. It takes great faith to share the gospel: it *is* divisive—God promises it to be, and others *will* consider our belief foolish.[1] It *can* make us nervous—they might not respond well; they might laugh at us. And it *is* intrusive—the cross draws a line between beliefs. Such is Christian experience, throughout history and across the world. But the faith by which Paul and the righteous live isn't faith in others' perspective of us, or the relationship we have with them. It's faith in a far greater God than those idols. And that faith caused Paul—and causes us—not to be ashamed of the gospel.

Eboo Patel started Interfaith Youth Core, which works primarily on college campuses. Eboo—a Muslim who I (Bob) admire deeply and love—once asked what I believed. "Eboo, I'd never offend you in the world, but I really believe based on the Bible that Jesus is God's Son and the only way to the Father." I told him of working in Vietnam and later in Afghanistan with Muslims. He told me one of the reasons he partnered with us is because I held to my faith and still wanted a relationship with him.[2] People do not just want honesty, but clarity to understand what we believe. It's a matter of how we say it. I've become convinced that truth is always kind and humble. Harshness, mean-spiritedness and arrogance often display insecurity about our beliefs. If we believe the truth, we should be the most secure, humble, compassionate people on earth. We have nothing to be ashamed of.

CHRISTIANITY IN EVERYDAY CONVERSATIONS

We're not encouraging forcing God into every conversation, at the exclusion of everything else; that will ensure a "no" the next time you invite them over. We *are* encouraging allowing our faith to be a part of our normative, unforced conversation. Just like other parts of our lives are. Sharing the gospel begins by not omitting parts of our lives that speak to our beliefs. If your boss asks what you're doing this weekend, instead of "yard work and a birthday party Saturday, then some other stuff on Sunday before I watch the game," simply acknowledge that "some other stuff" means "going to a church gathering, and even serving on the parking team." If a neighbor wants your opinion on a hot-button issue, instead of simply talking about politics and human rights, bring your Higher Authority into the conversation.

Tim Keller said it like this: "You have to be willing to talk about how your faith integrates with your life. Because if you're in non-superficial relationships with people, your faith simply has to come up! Why you do this and why you do that, and why you don't do this and why you don't do that, and how you were helped with a problem—you just have to mention it. It should be very natural . . . You have to have a lot of non-superficial relationships with not-yet-believers, and you also have to have a willingness to talk about your faith, and how it affects how you think and live."[3] Here are a few, among many, common ways to bring faith into common conversation:

→ Talk about your faith and community: speak of church, its gatherings and events, meaningful relationships, and God's work with excitement and joy; it raises intrigue.

→ Talk about our redemption stories: talking about our lives both before Jesus and after takes courage, but is deeply moving in its vulnerability. And talk about moments of brokenness and reconciliation in your life since He redeemed you. It shows that you're still not perfect, but that Jesus continues to redeem areas of pain, struggle, and disbelief.

→ Share the result of your faith: show people our true rest, joy, peace, and comfort in God alone, because of His ongoing work in us. How does faith impact your daily life?

→ Give God due credit: as you talk about good things in your life, rightly attribute those blessings to God, the giver of every gift.

→ Point to the bigger story: as we discuss conflict, sin, pain, and brokenness in the world, or as we discuss success, joy, and echoes of redemption, acknowledge that every specific act is part of a larger story of brokenness and redemption.

→ Be generous with praise: whether watching a mountain sunrise or hearing a coworker complain about her assistant, point to beautiful things God has uniquely put in them.

→ Show great grace: instead of engaging in gossip, and instead of interacting with someone who's failed or hurt us, display the grace God first showed us.

→ Share our true thoughts when asked: instead of avoiding advice, or downplaying the fact that the gospel drives us, boldly give answers from a faith-filled worldview.

→ Don't talk about God differently with not-yet-believers than we do with believers: we normally talk openly about God, faith, and even struggles and doubt with our community; do the same in our mission field. Honesty and openness shows others we don't have every answer.

The gospel is important to us. While we talked earlier about listening well (see Day 18), the other side is equally true: to really get to know people, they need to know what's important to us. You talk about everything else in your life that's important. Don't *stop* talking about the big game, the hit movie, or your big project. Just make sure they're in their place and don't ignore the bigger driving force in your life. Don't be ashamed of the gospel. In normal conversation, and early in the relationship, let people know we're followers of Jesus.

101 WAYS
TO DEMONSTRATE THE GOSPEL

83 Talk about God: Speak naturally about Him, faith, community, and convictions. Essentially, speak about God as normally as you would the other things you consider important in your life.

84 Ask what people think of God: Literally everyone considers that question, and most will answer. Even if some answers scare you, it's a way to see how others think about deep things.

85 Talk to not-yet-believers the same way you talk to Christians: Discuss hobbies, passions, work, or whatever you talk about in Christian circles—95 percent of conversation can look the same.

86 It's okay if God doesn't always come up: God, faith, and spirituality won't work themselves into every conversation. You'll have another chance. Enjoy time together without looking for the "open door" every moment.

"DEAR GOD . . ."

EVERY YEAR, GOD PUTS ME IN THE LIVES OF 50–100 STUDENTS WHO WOULDN'T WALK INTO BOB'S CHURCH, MINE, OR ANY OTHER.

One of my greatest joys of teaching at TCU is the opportunity to meet, mold, and teach not-yet-believers. While I'm open about my faith, I don't pray before each class sessions begin; I don't pray for their exams—at least not out loud. But every semester, I divide my classes into groups of three or four and meet students for lunch. It's a way to get to know them, learn how I can serve them, and to lay a foundation for future relationship. Before we eat, many times I'll pause and simply say that as a Christian, I believe all things are from God. I ask if anyone would be offended if I thank Him for the food. In ten semesters, not one student has said "no." I'll admit I'm nervous asking some students; I've chickened out more than once. But a simple prayer can not only thank God for His gifts of food and much more, but can also remember His generous provision, creativity in taste, care for us, and physical nourishment. In these things, I thank Him honestly and out loud, for the ways all these elements point toward His greatest provision, creativity, care, and deeper nourishment, which are all found most fully in Jesus. They're simple prayers, then

ANSWER
We share the gospel as we pray for—and with—others

READ
1 Kings
18:20–46

we get on with lunch. But students have heard the gospel declared, and have seen that faith makes a difference.

In addition to praying *for* our mission fields (see Day 14), one way to declare the gospel is to pray publicly, *with* those in our mission fields. Elijah's example may be an odd one to point to today. We're not suggesting praying for fire, building altars, or slaughtering either cows or false prophets. But in this instance—like other prophetic moments as well as Jesus' and His apostles' prayers before healing[4]—Elijah publicly invoked the Lord, who then revealed His power and truth in a meaningful way, and people believed in Him. Today we walk a fine line. We're not exploiting moments and mindsets in the lives of not-yet-believers. But as we look for ways to share the gospel without killing the relationship, prayer is one practically helpful and God-honoring answer.

PRAYER HONORS PEOPLE

At first glance, praying with not-yet-believers may seem odd. After all, they don't believe what we believe, why would they want us to pray with them? We've found over and over that—even if they don't believe in any higher being—prayer is often perceived as a means of honor. People might respond to your request to pray for them, "Sure, that would be nice." Even if their honest thought is, "I think you're crazy, but I'm honored you're willing to consider me in your silly belief in some big man in the sky. So why not?" They may see our prayers as fantasy; they might write them off as quaint tradition. But if nothing else, it's a thoughtful gesture. Pausing to show concern helps them feel valued, whether they believe in our methods or not.

We (Bob and Niki) have had nearly a hundred exchange students live with us. Ti, a Vietnamese student, was agnostic. After he moved in I said, "Ti, we are glad you're here, but we thank God for our food. We're going to pray over every meal. You don't have to. You can think about Buddha, Ho Chi Minh, or nothing. But we are going to pray and if there is anything we need to pray about with you, we are happy to." After high school he studied at TCU, and was with us for holidays and many weekends. We now think of him as a son. One of the last times he was here, he asked if he could pray. He didn't even believe in God. But he prayed. It was a special moment. I've prayed with not-yet-believers in mosques, hospitals, and meetings with some of the world's leading diplomats. One thing I've learned: even if people don't believe in God or not your God, they value prayer.

If praying with someone once is meaningful, following up is even more meaningful. Revisiting the prayer request days or weeks later acknowledges we listened to them, heard their need, pain, or joy, and have joined them in it since the initial prayer. Many of us aren't great about following up with prayer requests. "I'll pray for that" is often merely a Christian way to say, "I acknowledge your concern." What if we actually trusted God—and honored our neighbors—by submitting their needs, welfare, pains, and salvation to the only God who can meet, provide, overcome, and save? We're not encouraging a daily check-in call, but rather an intentional follow-up next time you see them. Or simply see if there's anything else you can do periodically. When we remember a big moment or need in someone's life, we show that we know and care for them.

NATURAL TIMES FOR PRAYER

Over time, Bobby had become known as "the Christian" on his block. Everyone knew Bobby would pray for them, serve them, bend over backward for them. After all, he and his family had done so for nearly everyone on his block. So when their subdivision lost a beloved neighbor, everyone gravitated toward Bobby's house, without even being asked. They knew he would pray and lead the charge in caring for them and their newly widowed neighbor. Prayer is natural—even expected—in situations like this. In such moments, prayer is an unforced way to publicly declare our faith, and to point others to the gospel. Here are three opportunities—common to everyone on earth—to declare truth through prayer, even if those we're with don't believe what we believe.

Praise and Thanksgiving

Rather than praising someone else for an accomplishment, praise God from Whom all blessings flow. Rather than celebrating ourselves for making it through another year in a birthday toast, thank the Giver of every good and perfect gift. When we get a raise, have a child, win an award, or experience other thanks-worthy moments in life, let's give credit where credit is due. And when not-yet-believers experience the same things, our equally-God-focused responses display that we not only rest in God, His favor, and His provision in our own lives, but also in theirs.

Tragedy and Joy

A sad, true reality exists in our broken world: everyone faces tragedy. And an equally great, true reality exists in our grace-filled world: everyone finds joy. Seasons of both occur in everyone's life. Both extremes offer moments to pray with people; to "rejoice with those who rejoice, [and] weep with those who weep."[5] In tragedy, we might pray that God the Spirit would bring the comfort and peace that only He can. We might pray that He reveal how the tragedy might be used for good. We might simply admit that we don't understand, but we trust Him and thus find rest. In joy, we declare Him to be better than whatever situation or honor, and thank Him for His grace and favor.

Need and Direction

Knowing those in our mission field well means we know when they have a need. Sometimes the need is financial; sometimes it's for healing—physical or otherwise. Or maybe they're at a life juncture—like everyone faces at times—and need to know the best next step. Submitting their needs to God, or praying that He would direct their steps, can be a scary but meaningful time of prayer. I am often awed at the faith of, say, Moses or Jesus' disciples, who prayed that God would bring forth water or heal someone's lameness.[6] What a potential embarrassment they set themselves up for, in front of a massive crowd! But as they prayed, God displayed His power, and turned hearts toward Him. We can pray for God to meet needs and give direction, whether through miraculous or everyday ways. And we must even be willing to be part of His answer, as He calls us.

OUR VIEW OF PRAYER, REGARDLESS OF THEIRS

We're not relegating prayer to merely a tool for God's mission. Regardless of what *they* think of it, as believers *we* know that prayer is, among other things, an act of obedience, a display of reliance, a means by which God displays His power, and a way to surrender our will to God's.[7] Prayer is vital for Christian life. Prayer is primarily about God, and that fact gives us boldness to pray, no matter who is in our midst. But we also don't want to ignore that public prayer is also vital for mission. At very least, prayer is one way by which God

101 WAYS TO DEMONSTRATE THE GOSPEL

87 Pray before a meal: Simply explain that you believe food to a blessing from God, and that you want to offer thanks. Offer thanks and ask God to bless your companion(s), then move on.

88 If prayer offends them, don't: On the complete other end of the spectrum, if praying would kill the relationship, skip the previous suggestion and still enjoy your food as a blessing, given by God.

89 Submit needs to the true Provider: Tell them you'll pray for their pain, struggles, or need. If they ask why, explain your view of God's ability to meet every need. If they'll let you, pray on the spot.

90 Talk about things you're thankful for: Make this a regular rhythm—not just at Thanksgiving. Take time to pause and rightly direct your thanks for the things for which you're grateful.

carries out His sovereign will.[8] Let us elevate both private and public prayer; let us pray for and with our mission fields.

One of the greatest moments in my TCU career came in an email from a former student: "You know I don't believe what you believe. But I'm dealing with a family tragedy, and don't have anyone to turn to. I think you told us you were a priest or something, so I wondered if I could come talk with you." After I chuckled at his perception of me as a priest—in the clerical sense—I was overcome with the blessing of the email. For semesters I'd shared my faith, prayed for students, and prayed with them. And God was bearing fruit in this student, as in others before and since, through persistence, patience, and both private and public prayer.

D—FENCE! D—FENCE!

IT WAS MAYBE THE BIGGEST "MISSIONAL FAILURE" OF MY LIFE.

Jim was my best friend and college roommate, and I had no idea where he stood with God. He was a reserved, thoughtful guy, so I was completely caught off guard the day he asked out-of-the-blue, "Ben, do you think I'm a Christian?" Startled and puzzled, I stuttered and danced around a few thoughts to fill the awkward silence, and then choked out, "Yeah . . . um . . . probably." That was it. He caught me off guard. But at the time, it was one of precious few times Jim opened the door to a deep conversation. I blew it. I regretted it for months, looked for ways to reengage, and even tried leading questions once in a while, to see if the door would reopen. But for a couple years, it didn't.

Earlier in this book we looked at the flow of 1 Peter: the apostle encourages us to live out our identity in Christ, then shows us what that looks like. In the midst of encouraging a gospel response to even our suffering, he gives another way to share the gospel: prepare "a ready defense."

EVENTUALLY SOMEONE WILL ASK

Peter says that as we live a holy life; as we pursue faith among the Gentiles; as we respond to marriage, authorities, and even suffering in the power of the gospel, people will be curious.

ANSWER
We share the gospel through a "ready defense"

READ
1 Peter 3:13–16

As we live strange lives, and make choices that are illogical if not outright crazy, eventually someone will ask about it. The question can come a hundred different ways: "I don't get it . . ." or, "What's wrong with you?" Possibly they'll ask what we believe about a topic. Like Jim, they'll blurt, "Do you think I'm a Christian?" Or maybe it'll come from a child: Charlotte asked me last week, "Does God live inside me?" (How esoteric and theological do I get, without freaking her toddler brain out?) As we shine the light of Christ into the darkness of unbelief, people in the darkness see the light. So at some point, someone will ask about your life and your faith. What do we do when that happens?

At a dinner in Doha, Qatar, with Jews, Muslims, secular Christians, and atheists, I (Bob) was asked to explain the Trinity. A little easier question would have been nice. Thankfully, I'd been asked that several times before and was able to answer. At that same meeting I wound up eating a meal with some members of the Taliban. They asked about Jesus and I explained what I believed. My answers are beside the immediate point: I share this story because a good friend—an atheist—who was eavesdropping later commented, "You know Bob, this is not just your religion. It's who you are, isn't it?" I'd be hard-pressed to find a more honoring comment.

WHAT IS A READY DEFENSE?

Peter's recommendation is to be ready; to put in the work *before* we have to explain why we're willing to suffer, forgive so easily, and don't sob when the economy takes a downturn. We prepare in advance to tell people what drives us to *that choice*, leads us to serve on the PTA of a downtrodden school, or a million other things. Today we ask you to think through your own explanation of your faith. A ready defense is the way to explain your personal hope in Christ, in a way that others understand. Today's verses give a few parameters for crafting a defense: it's hopeful, personal, succinct, gentle, and respectful.

A Hopeful, Personal Defense

The entire reason our lives look abnormal is that we rest in a different hope than the world. If our hope were in money, we'd be in shambles when the economy is, and overly elated at an unexpected year-end bonus—just like everyone around us. If your spouse exists solely to make you happy, you're frustrated and unforgiving when he or she doesn't—just like everyone else. A "ready defense" clearly explains why you put your hope in Jesus. The defense is of *your own* faith, so it will be personal. It's not a list of objective facts; it's about God's work in *you*, which gives *you* greater hope than anything else does. Think through the things you put your hope in before Jesus: how did each let you down? How did Jesus enter your life, and prove Himself a better foundation? What promises did He fulfill that nothing else did? Hopefully these are worshipful questions: you're recalling the moment God redeemed you from death to life. That is the basis for a hopeful defense.

A Succinct Defense

Explaining our hope in Jesus may not be the most difficult part of a ready defense; more difficult might be explaining it before someone loses interest or gets confused. The gospel is a diamond; its nuanced glories are revealed from each unique angle. The full character of God cannot be explained in a year, much less a few seconds. But even theologian J. I. Packer has summarized the gospel as succinctly as three words: "God saves sinners."[9] Your defense won't likely be that brief, but neither can it take an hour. We must explain enough of the gospel, and its impact on our lives, in the time we normally take to answer a question—between several seconds and a few minutes.

A Gracious, Respectful Defense

Peter encourages our defense to be gentle and respectful, so people can't accuse us of being rowdy, argumentative, or riot-causing. To pick up a theme of our book, both gentle-ness and respect ask us to humble ourselves and consider the perspective of the person asking. Gentleness and re-spect turn us away from picking a fight. They dissuade us from turning the conversation around to attack their faith. We cannot slam the open door of opportunity in their face, reject or mock their questions, or intellectually prove our-selves superior. Gentleness and respect lead us to respond and defend, but to do so with much love and grace.

This posture prevents us from quoting lots of verses, be-cause they likely don't believe the Bible. It causes us to avoid big theological words, because those confuse or demean them. It keeps us humble instead of haughty. God's grace and love toward us rightly motivates our own grace and love toward those God sent us to. Our ready defense should dis-

101 WAYS TO DEMONSTRATE THE GOSPEL

91 Introduce yourself: Linger outside instead of immediately shutting your garage door; cross the street. Be intentional with con-versation at work or school; don't be silent.

92 Talk about books or movies: Instead of working on a flight or stuffing headphones in on the bus, publicly read books or watch movies that start conversation. Or ask what they're reading or watching.

93 Activities culti-vate conversa-tion: Board games are fun and reveal competitiveness. Songwriter circles dis-play pain and passion as you shape each other's craft. Book clubs, baking, beer- or wine-tasting, and knit-ting invite you to enjoy the activity and talk.

94 Help neighbors—and admit your own needs: From the stereotypi-cal cup of sugar to your time, bless your neighbors. And turn to them for help as well: create a culture of uninhibited sharing.

play the gospel, even as we declare it. We demonstrate the character of God, even as we stand up for our faith.

WHAT'S YOUR READY DEFENSE?

We end today with our own stories we keep tucked away, in case anyone asks about our faith. Here's a common way I explain the gospel's work in me: "I knew I was a broken man, but for as long as I can remember, I looked to my own achievements and girls as my greatest satisfaction. When those both let me down, I realized just how broken I was. I tried to fix the brokenness myself, in every way I knew how. But nothing worked. Thankfully, God did what I couldn't, and redeemed me by the death and resurrection of Jesus. He promises a joy and restoration I could never find for myself. That joy and promise impacts how I see everything in my life." And here's mine (Bob's): "I was a moral and religious person from an early age. But I grew up seeing people that were genuine in their faith and others that weren't. I wasn't sure what made a person real in God. But in reading the Sermon on the Mount, one day I realized that God had a different way of living. I told God I wanted to live like that sermon, and know Him like they knew Him in the Bible. It changed my life."

Two perspectives; two unique lives changed by one glorious God. They're probably not perfect or complete examples. You cynics can pick them both apart. Neither covers every facet of the gospel. Neither is rich in theology, Bible, or big words. But they're honest. And they try to show hopelessness, hope, and Jesus who makes the eternal difference between the two. In our own lives.

Those are our succinct, hopeful, and personal ready defenses; what's yours?

DAY 29

OBJECTIVE GOSPEL; SUBJECTIVE LIVES

"I DO DRUGS. WHAT WOULD JESUS SAY ABOUT THAT?"

ANSWER
We share the gospel by applying it to everyday situations

READ
Ephesians
4:11–16

Here's a scenario for you: you're a night security guard and the only Christian on duty. Another guard suddenly sticks his head into your office. Pointing his finger he almost accuses, "You're one of those 'Christians,' right?" Nothing good ever follows that question. No one gives you a high five, says "Good job," and goes about their business. They want to debate, challenge, or stump you. You hesitantly respond, "Yeah . . ." He crosses his arms, looks you square in the eye and then comes the challenge: "I do drugs. What would Jesus say about that?" How would you respond—in a way that might actually resonate?

THREE INSUFFICIENT RESPONSES

I've posed this scenario, which actually happened to a guy I know named Nick, in trainings around the country. No matter where I am, I hear these responses:

"Um, I don't know exactly."

For some, our gut response would be to look down, stammer, and ashamedly admit we don't know what Jesus would say. Maybe it's the outlandish honesty or the shock of a challenge at two a.m. Perhaps we have a hard time putting Jesus' response into words. Or our people-pleaser kicks in and we simply can't tell him the core of what we believe. A common response to this question is a blank stare. Put yourself in the shoes of the asker: "I don't know" looks like ignorance.

"He'd tell you to stop."

For others, the answer would stem from the moralistic, humanist culture we grew up in. Our answer is some form of Bob Newhart's MADtv sketch,[10] where a counselee admits a number of struggles, while Newhart "counsels" each with a blunt, "Stop it!" Even if we intellectually know Jesus is our Savior, we function as if He is a good guy with ethical advice. Maybe we advise a few "good works." Perhaps we appeal to legality ("You'll get arrested"), personal welfare ("It might kill you"), heartstrings ("If you get arrested, can you imagine how your family will feel?"), or moralism ("You know it's wrong"). It could be that we even quote a verse: "He'd say, 'You shall have no other gods before me'; that's the first commandment." Put yourself in the asker's shoes again: "Stop it" fits a view of God many already assume: a rule-giving, demanding, and impersonal deity.

"He died for your sin so you can be with Him in heaven."

A final common response acknowledges their need for the gospel. Maybe you've been praying for this guard. You're elated that God finally opened the door. So you gush the gospel many of us know well. "He'd tell you that God is perfect and heaven is perfect, but because of sin, you're not perfect. God sent Jesus to die for your sin so you can be reconciled to God and live eternal life with Him. If you accept Jesus He'll forgive your sin of drugs." This is true—and praise God it is! But if he's ignoring God, he doesn't care about heaven. If he's like much of the world, he doesn't believe he's too bad a person. If he's a common American, it's likely he doesn't fully understand sin or his need for Jesus. Even the objective, big-picture gospel is not a sufficient answer.

"LIKE CHILDREN, TOSSED TO AND FRO . . ."

These responses fail to get to the heart of our faith. The first is empty; the second is moralistic. The third sees the gospel as merely a past event that greatly benefits my future, but that has nothing to do with today. Many who question the gospel need to know how it applies to them in their current situation. Behind the challenging question is a heart in need of applicable truth.

Futile attempts like these are not unique to our culture. Writing to first-century Ephesus, Paul explains the goal of Christian life is maturity, then gives three ways we cannot attain that goal: "Every wind of doctrine, by human cunning, by craftiness in deceitful schemes."[1] First, exclusively pursuing doctrinal trends, teachers, or head-knowledge of the Bible isn't enough. Second, we will always be let down by relying on our own power, to make new rules and fix each other. Third, false teachers deceive, spouting false hope and false ways to solve real issues.

But these are ways we often answer many questions, not just the two a.m. drug challenge. "How can God redeem my broken marriage?" "I'm so angry at my boss, what do I do?" "We just want a baby." "How do these verses or commands apply to me?" "Where is God in this recent tragedy?" We answer, "I don't know" (and if you're really good, ". . . but I'll pray for you."). "Let me give you a great book on that." "Let's meet every week for accountability." "Do these three things or steps." "You just need to trust Jesus." "One day, all this will be better."

APPLYING AN OBJECTIVE GOSPEL TO SUBJECTIVE SITUATIONS

None of these, Paul would say, are sufficient for faith or maturity. He even calls answers like this childlike. Answers like these miss one of the great blessings of the gospel. It *is* a past event, both historically and personally for every Christian. It *does* give future hope, for personal reconciliation and the renewal of all things. But it *also* impacts every moment of our present lives. The gospel means something, to everyone, every day, for every situation, whether they know it or not. Paul says that while those other ways fail, the one way to grow in Christ is to "speak the truth in love."[12]

This is why we listen well; why we learn stories. Within every complaint, struggle, and idol hides an opportunity to speak the objective truth of the gospel into someone's subjective circumstance. Jeff Vanderstelt offers four areas to listen for, in every story, frustration, and situation, where we can intervene and point people toward Jesus:[13]

→ Identity: Who or what shapes their understanding of themselves? Where do they find personal value and worth, instead of God?

→ Brokenness: Where are things "different" than they're supposed to be? What are areas of pain, hurt, and frustration? Who or what do they blame, instead of sin?

→ Redemption: What or who do they look to, to fix the brokenness? What or who makes everything right? What or who is their functional redeemer, instead of Jesus?

→ Hope: What does "right" look like? What would everything look like once everything is fixed? What or who is the center of that hope, instead of Jesus?

When we identify false identity or hope in someone's life, see a misplaced view of brokenness, or hear the letdown of a false redeemer, we can point them toward a better story. We lead them to an identity and hope in God, not anything or anyone else. We define sin as the true brokenness, not any other problem. We point to Jesus as the only true Redeemer in the midst of the siren calls of false saviors. That loves them well, and speaks gospel truth in a way that addresses a direct need.

HOW WOULD YOU RESPOND?

"I do drugs. What would Jesus say about that?" Based on today's content, how do we answer that question? What deeper need do the drugs really cover? What true struggle is he admitting? Put yourself in Nick's shoes: how does the objective gospel apply to the guard's subjective situation?

After thinking for a moment, Nick responded, "I think Jesus would tell you you're looking for hope in a place that lets you down. And you know it lets you down because you have to take a hit three times a day. So I think Jesus would tell you He's a better place to put your hope, because He promises He'll never let you down." Nick spoke the gospel truth into the basis of the guard's personal hope. In thousands of years of history, sixty-six biblical books, and millions of lives across history, God has proven that Jesus is our greatest hope. The guard didn't fall on his knees weeping that night. God didn't redeem his soul in that office. But he uncrossed his arms, shook his head, and told Nick, "No one has ever told me that before. That actually makes a lot of sense." That night, the guard walked having heard the gospel in a way that resonated with his present life and need.

101 WAYS
TO DEMONSTRATE THE GOSPEL

95 Practice the "one anothers": Realizing your own imperfection helps you develop grace for others' imperfections. Have those around you encourage, exhort, rebuke, and correct you.

96 See the gospel applies in every facet of life: You'll have a hard time applying it to their situation if you've never considered your own. What do you disbelieve about God in your fear, anger, laziness, misplaced joy, hopes, etc.?

97 Apply the gospel with other believers: Many have been taught not to meddle; to leave them alone. But if we can't speak the gospel to other believers' situations, there's far less likelihood we'll do it with those who don't yet believe.

JUST DO IT

TEN THOUSAND HOURS

In *Outliers*, **that's** how much intentional practice sociologist Malcolm Gladwell claims it takes to master a skill or subject.[14] I've seen this proven true with preaching, speaking Spanish, and playing piano, among other things. I started piano lessons in kindergarten, and other than a short hiatus near the beginning of high school played through my senior year. At this peak of my piano career, if you will, I went to Texas's All-State Competition playing a Debussy solo. I didn't win. But making it to state was a great honor—which only came with tons of practice. "Dr. Gradus ad Parnassum" is a rapid-fire, flowing gush of beauty. It took over seven months to learn, memorize, and nuance the performance.[15] Seven months, in the midst of school, part-time jobs, over-involvement, and trying to "live it up" my last year of high school. But the practice was worth it.

SHARE THE GOSPEL FOR 10,000 HOURS?!

A similar theme runs through the Bible: ministry takes practice. The apostles spent years with Jesus, but it took them a while to "get" who He was and what they were doing. Mark gives us a glimpse of Demon Casting 101, when they tried all they knew but were unable to cast out a certain type of demon.[16] From the prophet Samuel's childhood training with the priest Eli, to

ANSWER
We learn to share the gospel by practicing sharing the gospel

READ
Romans 8:18–25

Timothy, Silas, and others apprenticing with Paul, we see that any ministry takes practice, trial, and error.[17]

Sharing the gospel is not a skill to acquire or a subject area to master. So we are not suggesting you must share the gospel for one hour each day for the next 27.3 years. But as with anything on earth, the more you share the gospel, the easier it becomes to share the gospel. Sure, some people might find it easy, and certainly, with God all things are possible. But for many of us, if Gladwell is right— and if the experience of any musician, speaker, athlete, or person-good-at-anything-under-the-sun confirms his theory—one way we share the gospel is to practice. A lot. To try it and fail. To get nervous, sweat, and stutter. To feel like you've landed the perfect point, only to meet a stone cold response. To feel like you blew it, only to see someone cry like a baby, realizing their need for Jesus. And everything in-between.

ORDINARY PEOPLE, EXTRAORDINARY GOSPEL

This last stop on our thirty-day journey spotlights people like you. We want to show you ways that workers, students, parents, and artists have shared the gospel in everyday ways. Through these real-life examples, like Nick's story yesterday, consider your own life. Today's verses remind us that every human life, and every aspect of God's creation, exists in brokenness and yearns for redemption. Since everything on earth reflects God's story, common situations can point to needs that Jesus meets, and ordinary conversations are opportunities to share the gospel. Some names below are real; some aren't (some relationships are developing so we're being sensitive to the individuals and their missions). And each story fits in a broader conversation. These snapshots rob them of nuance and context. If something strikes you as odd, bold, or cheesy, know there's more to each story. By God's grace, the gospel made an impact, in a unique way at that unique moment. Just like it does with people you talk to, in surprising ways.

Anne shared the gospel with a fellow auditor, starting with a company's ledger. The goal of the financial records was to be correct, but incorrect numbers meant the books were broken. Being numbers and formulas, they could not fix themselves, but the books needed to be reconciled (poignant word, no?). Anne explained that by sacrificing time and effort to find and fix the problem, auditing the books reflected Jesus' work in each of our lives: we're broken and can't fix ourselves, so Jesus comes, sacrifices, and reconciles us to God.

Scared, angry, and confused, a coworker turned to Stew for advice after getting his girlfriend pregnant. Stew talked about the beauty of life, God's creation and perfect design for their baby, and how God alone gave Stew himself the power to be a good dad. He shared promises of God: He works for His objective good, and He inconvenienced Himself to give His people true life. Stew's coworker is not yet a believer, but he and his girlfriend decided to keep the baby and get married, and his relationship with Stew has increased.

Kristy shared the gospel in the aftermath of a difficult break-up. By comparing her friend's false hope in the man she so desperately wanted but who let her down regularly, to true hope in Jesus who will never let her down, she pointed out the deficiencies in her friend's idol.

Mark has shared the gospel by considering the seasons of the year. The earth goes through a rhythm of death and rebirth to remain healthy. But the earth cannot die and rebirth itself; it relies on something outside itself. Whether the angle of the sun, precipitation and wind, or (more rightly) God, the seasons reflect what God does in us: we're dying day by day, but God makes us new. Another friend uses nature too, seeing the rhythm of day to night and back.

Jen shared the gospel at her husband's funeral. He died suddenly and earlier than logic would expect, and she told of his love for her but mostly of his love for God. Then she tearfully declared that her solace in the midst of grief: was knowing her husband was in God's presence. She shared about her own life without Jesus, then with Jesus; about death without Jesus, then with Jesus. Then she implored the hundreds gathered to follow her husband's example and live for Jesus.

Jess shares the gospel as she disciplines Charlotte and Maggie. Instead of simply punishing them, she sees situations through a gospel lens. "Do you know why you're in trouble?" "What was the right thing to do?" Instead of simply encouraging better behavior, Jess asks if they know why it's so hard to obey. She explains that our hearts are selfish and sinful, but God helps us obey when we don't want to. She reminds them that Mommy and Daddy love them, that our role is to point them to God, and that discipline is a way to help get back on the right path. After they repeat, "Mommy, I'm sorry I (whatever). Will you forgive me?" Then we celebrate forgiveness with laughter and hugs, and thank God for the ability to obey. Neither Maggie nor Charlotte follow Jesus yet. But in this way, Jess shares the gospel with them regularly—sometimes a few times each week!

SEEING THE GOSPEL IN EVERY ORDINARY THING

As part of creation, music yearns for resolution to its dissonance. From fiction to dramas; from *Braveheart* to romantic comedies, the best stories start out good (Scotland is free or a romance develops). Then brokenness enters the plot (England takes over or the dude blows it and they break up), and all they want is to make it right again. If Scotland wasn't free by the end credits of *Braveheart*, or if the couple isn't making out on the Brooklyn Bridge while violins swell in the background, audiences consider it a horrible movie. But something always has to initiate that resolution, most often not the parties involved. William Wallace had to lead the Scottish army to "freedom!"; the best friend has to step in and help the dude realize he's a moron.[18] The gospel is echoed in most story lines, whether on a screen, page, or stage. Or move from art to real life: we know too well broken relationships, bodies, families, holiness, or dreams. We're familiar with deep longings. The same longings everyone feels are one aspect of "not only the creation, but we ourselves . . . groan inwardly as we wait eagerly for adoption as sons, the redemption of our bodies."[19] We have a mutual starting point to speak good news into someone's life.

What do you do for a living? What need does it meet, and how does that echo a greater need that only Jesus can meet? What brokenness exists in your life, and how is Jesus the only hope for that situation? What hobby, natural phenomenon, or entertainment do you enjoy, and how does its beauty, story, awe-inspiring reality, or other attribute declare the glory of God, in its everyday being? What questions are being asked, or emotions displayed, and what's the deeper struggle behind that question or emotion? These are specific souls. These are each single situations. But as you take a deep breath, pray for strength and wisdom, and give it a whirl, you take steps toward sharing the gospel without killing the relationship. You'll get more comfortable. You'll get more confident. You'll find ways you didn't realize before—simply by thinking, practicing, and doing it.

101 WAYS
TO DEMONSTRATE THE GOSPEL

98 Over-explain Christian practices: As you bring not-yet-believing friends into the life of believing friends, things like prayer, Bible passages, and communion are teaching moments: explain each and why it's important.

99 Watch your reactions: Respond to small frustrations in gracious ways. Ignore office gossip. Display patience in difficulty. The "small moments" of life are platforms to display your faith.

100 Go deep: Be proactive and go beyond surface-level conversations. Ask "Why?" Get to the heart of the matter. Show people you truly care, and be willing to admit your own messes too.

101 Give yourself grace: This applies to every bit of this book, so it's a good one to end on. When—not if!—you mess up, misrepresent God, offend someone, speak truth without love, or even botch the gospel, give yourself grace. Jesus was the only perfect human; the rest of us are in the process of being transformed into His likeness. And transformation is a long road!

"HOW" QUESTIONS FOR YOU TO WORK THROUGH

☐ **GENERAL:** What impacted you the most this week? What was new, convicting, or confusing? What was difficult? What do you need to discuss with others?

☐ **GENERAL:** Where's your heart, as you consider God's mission? What are you currently thinking? What's motivating you? What scares you? How is God moving in you?

☐ **DAY 26:** What are some of the things that you find important, and talk about often? If you say Jesus is more important than those, why don't you talk about faith?

☐ **DAY 26:** Think through the past few days' conversations: what are some natural moments that you could have mentioned something about God?

☐ **DAY 27:** Have you ever prayed in front of someone who didn't know Jesus? If not, why not? If so, how did they respond?

☐ **DAY 27:** What are some situations in your normal week that you could pray for and with others? Who are some people in your mission field you should pray with?

☐ **DAY 28:** Have you ever been asked about your faith—to explain it, defend it, describe it, etc.? How did you respond? If "not well," what hindered it?

☐ **DAY 28:** Take some time and prayerfully work through a hopeful, personal, succinct, gracious, and respectful explanation of your faith in Christ (See p. 195 for our own examples)

☐ **DAY 29:** Consider your own heart. If you cannot apply the gospel to your subjective situations, it's difficult to apply it to others. In what things do you find your identity and hope, other than Jesus? What do you define as the problem in a given situation, and what do you look to, to solve it? How might the gospel be "good news" to each of those subjective situations?

☐ **DAY 29:** Think of various people in your mission field: in what things does each find their identity and hope, other than Jesus? What do they define as the problem in a given situation, and what do they look to, to solve it? How might the gospel be "good news" in each subjective situation?

☐ **DAY 30:** Who are Christians in your life with whom you can practice sharing the gospel? Have them push back, or present you with different scenarios, and practice speaking the good news.

☐ **DAY 30:** The gospel story is echoed everywhere; we just need to notice it. What are normal elements, objects, moments, or tasks in your job, hobby, home, etc. that could be starting points for gospel conversations? Practice sharing the gospel from each of these starting points.

☐ **GENERAL:** Look back over this week's "Everyday Mission Ideas." What additional, practical things can you come up with, specific to your personality, gifting, and mission field, to live out God's mission? Share your ideas online with the hashtag #everydaymission.

MY MISSION
JEFF VANDERSTELT

TACOMA, WASHINGTON

"This is Jeff, that pastor I told you about who is not like a normal pastor," Amy said as she introduced me to Clay. Clay and Christie had children who attended our local elementary with Amy's children. Amy had told us many times that she didn't believe what we did. However, she regularly introduced us to her friends thinking they might be interested.

We'd lived in the neighborhood for three years with the intent of bringing good news to this community, and that the syllables and sentences were meant to be enfleshed. We started by hosting a cookout every Friday night. At first we were told people didn't do that in our neighborhood. However,

the kingdom of God has the power to break in and create a new culture. It happened. Dinner parties became more normative, as did other celebrations.

Typically we hosted the Halloween party, but this year our neighbors wanted to. Clay and I were outside in the damp Puget Sound night with the kids while the women stayed back. I asked Clay about himself, where and how he grew up, and what he loved. By the end of the evening, I had gained a new friend and an understanding of how to share the good news to him. Clay was a typical Northwesterner. He was looking for peace, light, and power but had no place for God at that point. He and Christie joined us for several dinner parties and nights out following our first meeting.

One night Clay asked if we would join him and his family for a weekend away at the coast. He had just come back in from surfing. "I love the ocean! The waves, the wind, the power I feel when I'm on my surfboard...I love it!" he said. Then he asked, "What do you think it is about the water? The power...why do I feel so connected to it?" I responded, "Well Clay, the power in the water is telling you what God is like. He created everything to point to His invisible attributes. God is powerful. The waves are directing you to Him. The problem, however, is that we all fail to give God credit and we worship His creation instead of what His creation is pointing to." "Well," he replied, "I don't know about that, but there's something there."

After we put our children to bed, we were sitting together in the hot tub. Clay broke the silence, "So, Christie and I want to let you know why we invited you to join us here. Our daughter, Emma, has been asking questions about God and we don't know what to tell her. What do we say?" The months of eating, celebrating, listening, and loving had built a foundation of trust. For several minutes I told God's redemption story through Jesus from the first creation to the new creation.

After that weekend, Clay and Christie started serving in our community garden. We had decided the best way to serve our widowed, hoarding neighbor was to turn her forest-like backyard into a garden for our neighborhood. I continued to tell Clay about God's kingdom, using the garden as a metaphor of God's plan to restore all things through the person and work of Jesus.

My fortieth birthday rolled around and Jayne planned an incredible party. The whole night was a beautiful picture of God's kingdom and a foretaste of the future party we will have with Jesus. At the end of the night, she invited people to toast me. Many in our missional community toasted to the ways they observed Jesus at work in and through my life. Amy, our neighbor, got up, raised her glass and said, "You know I don't believe what you believe. However, if I were ever to become a Christian, I would want to be like you, Jeff." I was blown away!

Clay stood up with his glass lifted high and said, "You and I have had many conversations about God and Jesus and stuff. I don't know what's going on, but I feel like I'm on the edge of a precipice . . . like something is drawing me . . . a power or a light or something like that. Whatever it is, it's in you. I've seen it. I've felt it. I've heard it when you talk. I toast to whatever that is."

Then I raised my glass. "This is an amazing evening. Thank you Jayne! We had a great time tonight eating, drinking, celebrating, and laughing. People from all backgrounds who don't all believe the same thing. Clay, what you've experienced in me is Jesus' Spirit working through me. That's the reason this party is so good. Only Jesus can make a party this great." I went on to share that Jesus lived, died and rose again to bring about life of another kind for all of us. "The greatest gift I could ever receive would be to have each of you come to know the love of Jesus personally because he is the greatest gift I have ever received. So, everyone raise your glass. I toast to Jesus Christ!"

Months later, Clay decided to come to our Easter gathering where I shared the good news of Jesus again. This time something changed. He couldn't tell me what it was right away, but he was different. Later that week he met me in the garden and told me he was changed. He believed the truths about Jesus and he now knew Jesus' Spirit was in him like it was in me.

JEFF VANDERSTELT is the visionary leader of the Soma Family of Churches, and also serves as one of the teachers and elders at Soma Tacoma. Jeff has a passion to see the Church equipped and released to live on Jesus' mission through gospel intentionality in all of life. wearesoma.com

END HERE: YOUR MISSION

"YOU'RE GOING TO TRY TO CONVERT ME, AREN'T YOU?"

We've covered a lot of ground in thirty days. But we're closing this book by coming full circle, and going back to the chairs at The Love Shack, eating bacon burgers with "Ben and Jerry" (like the ice cream company). Part of why this story bookends our, well, book, is that at the time of writing, Jerry still isn't a Christian. There's no "bow" on his story, even though everyone likes stories with bows. We don't get to wrap it up nicely and tuck it away and live happily ever after. I've known him for over three years, and he's a good friend. We spend time together; our families interact as often as busy schedules allow. He knows we're telling this story, and he celebrates with us because the level of conversation Jerry and I have had has been amazing. He knows what I think about his eternity, and he wrestles with it. He knows I've wept for him, and I've told him plainly that I want him to know Jesus. He even mused once, "I think I'll confess John 3:16 on my deathbed."

NOT-YET-BELIEVERS?

It's not up to me to save Jerry. We lack the ability to convict, redeem, and breathe life into others. We lack the power to dictate who spends eternity with God and who does not. That's God's role. What's our role? For some, it's street evangelism; for some it's pastoring; for some it's heading to a cross-cultural context. But for all of us—including you, whoever and wherever you are—it's everyday mission in the neighborhoods, workplaces, schools, and relationships God has sent you to.

We've used the term "not-yet-believer" throughout this book to refer to those who don't know Jesus. There are two intentional reasons for that: first, it's a hopeful term for those to whom we're on mission. From the thief on the cross next to Jesus, to Jerry who I pray *does* confess John 3:16 one day, the word "yet" reminds us it's never too late. Our right is not to give up or write people off. But if the first use of the "not-yet" gives us hope, the other use should sober us: one day, "at the name of Jesus *every* knee should bow, *in heaven and on earth and under the earth*, and *every* tongue confess that Jesus Christ is Lord, to the glory of God the Father."[1] Get that? One day Jesus will return and, *every single person WILL* believe He is Lord. But while some will believe "in heaven" and others "on earth," some will only believe "under the earth." This is biblical imagery for *Sheol*, or hell. One day God will make every "not-yet-believer" into a believer. But if they don't believe before death or Jesus' return, then those we claim to love—those to whom God sent us—will still believe, but will glorify God on the wrong side of eternity.

When Jesus rebukes the religious leaders of His day, He exhorts them, "Go and learn what this means, 'I desire mercy, and not sacrifice.' For I came not to call the righteous, but sinners."[2] He echoes the prophet Amos, through whom God says to Israel,

> "I hate, I despise your feasts,
>> and I take no delight in your solemn assemblies.
> Even though you offer me your burnt offerings and grain offerings,
>> I will not accept them;
> and the peace offerings of your fattened animals,
>> I will not look upon them.
> Take away from me the noise of your songs;
>> to the melody of your harps I will not listen.
> But let justice roll down like waters,
>> and righteousness like an ever-flowing stream."[4]

Sacrifice was a way God's people worshiped. God Himself created a system of sacrifice, along with "songs, assemblies, feasts, and offerings," for His people's gatherings. But through Jesus and Amos, God says "NO MORE. The songs you sing? I won't listen. Your assemblies and communal feasts? I despise them. The offerings? I won't accept them." Why would God say such a thing? Amos's chapters 4–6 make it clear: God's people gather, sing songs, and look pretty in some ways God tells them to. They seem so holy. But they don't love people. They ignore sinners; they ignore the needy; they don't serve those outside God's own people. They don't display mercy; they don't seek justice. They ignore their role as a "nation of priests." In a word, they look inward and upward, but they've stopped looking outward.

A CLOSING INDICTMENT AND CHALLENGE

Bob and I don't know that God would say anything different to many Christians today than He said in Amos. We don't know that we look any different from God's people, who gather, sing, and worship, but who ignore those God sent us to. This is the urgency that drove us to write this book. Will you pursue mercy over sacrifice? Will you look outward? Will you lay down your life, and follow Jesus into His everyday mission? Will you worship God by obeying His call to "go make disciples"? We earnestly hope that by God's power, you will.

Though we don't know you all, we're praying for you as we write these closing words: that God would give you Christ-centered motivation, unnatural boldness, disproportionate influence, intentional actions and words, and Spirit-filled wisdom, as you live in a way that could add to the pages of this book. You've seen mission as it played out in the Bible. You've read stories of normal, everyday people, of how they put this biblical mandate into practice. But now it's your turn. In your mission field, how will you put this biblical mandate into practice? What's your story?

NOTES

START HERE: FIVE QUESTIONS

1. http//: www.TCU360.com.
2. Falsely attributed to Francis of Assisi; see http://thegospelcoalition.org/blogs/tgc/2012/07/11/factchecker-misquoting-francis-of-assisi/.
3. Many lists exist around the Internet of "25 Ways" or "Top 10 Ways" to love neighbors, coworkers, etc. We've both read some in the past, so it's likely that others' ideas became embedded in our minds. We did not intentionally consider anyone else's work as we crafted the collection for this book. For more ideas like these 101, however, vergenetwork.org has compiled many lists from others into free resources to serve you well.

WEEK ONE: WHY SHOULD I EVEN CARE?

1. Richard Rodgers and Oscar Hammerstein II, "Do–Re–Mi," 1959, *The Sound of Music*, 20th Century Fox. Stage.
2. See for examples of each: Sinner: Romans 3:7, 1 Peter 4:8; idolater: Ephesians 5:5; of our flesh: Ephesians 2:8; darkness: John 12:35, Romans 2:9, Ephesians 5:8; slave: Galatians 4:7, 23; children of wrath: Ephesians 2:3.
3. Respectively, Romans 12:2; Ezekiel 36:26; Ephesians 5:8; 2 Corinthians 5:17; Ephesians 1:5; Romans 6:7; Colossians 2:13.
4. Romans 1:16–17; Ephesians 2:8–10.
5. Alison Hodgson, personal interview, November 2013. Used with permission.
6. See Genesis 1:11–26.
7. In order below, 1) Matthew 9:12; 2) Luke 15:7; 3) Luke 19:10; 4) John 3:16.
8. There is some debate on the actual number of nations in the world. This number per http://www.nationsonline.org/oneworld/countries_of_the_world.htm.
9. *Pay It Forward*, Warner Bros., 2000 Film.
10. Luke 19:10.
11. Isaiah 6:8.
12. Luke 9:3–4.
13. See Philippians 2:1–4.
14. Proverbs 29:25.
15. Gareth Cook, "The Power of Introverts: A Manifesto for Quiet Brilliance," *Scientific American*: Jan. 24, 2012, http://www.scientificamerican.com/article.cfm?id=the-power-of-introverts, accessed September 21, 2013.
16. Previous sentences: Jonah 3:3–4; 4:2–3; 4:10–11 respectively.
17. Jonah 2:9; see also Psalm 3:8; Revelation 7:10.
18. 1 Corinthians 10:31.
19. See especially Leviticus 1–7.

20. Exodus 19:3–6, italics added.

21. These questions adapted from just a few of Dr. David Powlison's so-called "X-Ray Questions," quoted in Timothy S. Lane and Paul David Tripp, *How People Change* (Greensboro, NC: New Growth Press, 2006), 162ff. I don't know of a better source for cutting to the heart and revealing idols, and highly recommend the questions.

22. See Matthew 25:14–30.

23. John 4:35.

WEEK TWO: WHO IS MY EVERYDAY MISSION FIELD?

1. Previous sentences: James 1:27 and 2:8, respectively.

2. Acts 1:8, italics added. I (Bob) call this overlap of God's missional call "glocal." For more on the concept, see Bob Roberts Jr, *Glocalization: How Followers of Jesus Engage a Flat World* (Grand Rapids: Zondervan, 2007), or visit glocal.net.

3. See Joseph H. Thayer, *Thayer's Greek-English Lexicon of the New Testament* (Peabody, MA: Hendrickson Publishers,1996), BibleWorks software v. 9, s.v. πλησίον.

4. For more on the medieval usage of "vocation": Pope John Paul II, *Familiaris Consortio*, 11.4 (http://www.vatican.va/holy_father/john_paul_ii/apost_exhortations/doc uments/hf_jp-ii_exh_19811122_familiaris-consortio_en.html); Gustaf Wingren, *Luther on Vocation* (Eugene, OR: Wipf & Stock, 2004); David L. Jeffrey, *A Dictionary of Biblical Tradition in English Literature* (Grand Rapids: Eerdmans, 1992). Additionally, we hadn't read this before we finished our manuscript, but Tim Keller's *Every Good Endeavor* (New York: Dutton, 2012) unpacks this concept—and expands on all of today's theme—incredibly well.

5. Colossians 3:23.

6. James 1:17.

7. Jeff Vanderstelt, "Unleashing Everyday People into God's Mission." Austin, TX: Verge Conference, February 2010, http://www.youtube.com/watch?v=FJgKJzdxgIo. accessed August 14, 2013.

8. Jeff Moss, "People in your Neighborhood?" Festival Attractions, Inc: 1969. For a list of episodes featuring the song, see http://muppet.wikia.com/wiki/The_People_in_ Your_Neighborhood_(song), accessed November 23, 2013.

9. Respectively and in the order in the list, 1) Leviticus 19:18; 2) Matthew 5:43; 3) Galatians 5:14; 4) James 2:8; 5) Matthew 19:19; 22:39; Mark 12:31; Romans 13:9; and 6) Luke 10:27–37.

10. See other uses of "neighbor" in the Old Testament Law and wisdom literature: the term often referred to the person next door (Exodus 3, 12, 20; Deuteronomy 19, 23, 27; Proverbs 3), or close enough to call on (Exodus 22; Deuteronomy 24), do evil against (Leviticus 18–19; Deuteronomy 5, 19; Psalm 15, 101), or simply annoy (Proverbs 25, 27). Jeremiah and Micah distinguish between "neighbor," "brother/sister" (closer relationship), and "friend" (less-close relationship: Jeremiah 6, 9, 23, 31, 34; Micah 7).

11. See for example, Deuteronomy 27; Psalm 28, 101; 146; Proverbs 3, 6, 11, 14.

12. Thanks to Matt Formby for helping with specific research and content development of today's topic.

13. http://www.dailyfinance.com/blog/2010/10/04/25-most-dangerous-neighbor hoods-2010/.

14. Ephesians 2:10.

15. Kevin DeYoung and Greg Gilbert, *What Is the Mission of the Church?* (Wheaton, IL: Crossway, 2011), 230.

16. Ibid, 224–27: these are the subheadings for chapter 9 of their book, which develops each thought more fully.

17. We see this throughout the Gospels.

18. Summarized from, and learn more at, http://thenetfw.com; accessed August 14, 2013.

19. See Matthew 28:18–20; Mark 16:15–16; Luke 24:46–49; John 20:21–22; Acts 1:8.

20. See Acts 11:19–26; Acts 13:1–3.

21. http://www.dfwinternational.org/demographics/, accessed January 30, 2014.

22. Learn more at http://dashnetwork.net.

23. See for example, Deuteronomy 4:9; Psalm 78, 103.

24. Previous sentences: see for example Matthew 7:9–11; 11:16–19, 11:25–26; 18:3–5. Jesus' brothers wrote the biblical books James and Jude.

25. See for example, Matthew 12:50; 1 Timothy 5:1–2; Hebrews 2:12–13; Ephesians 4:6; "brother" and "sister" as reference to fellow Christians; adoption imagery in Romans 8, Ephesians 1–2; the household qualification in eldership (1 Timothy 3); and reference to God our "father," throughout the New Testament.

26. See for example, Acts 16:34 and Acts 18:8.

27. Mike Breen, *Leading Kingdom Movements* (3DM: 2013), 121. For full development of the oikos concept see chapter 9 of the same. Stark's book referenced is *The Rise of Christianity* (San Francisco: Harper, 1997).

28. See *National Lampoon's Christmas Vacation*, Warner Bros, 1989 (unless you're easily offended by cheap, somewhat crass humor; if so then don't see it).

29. Exodus 20:12; 1 Peter 3:1–2; also see 1 Corinthians 7:14.

30. Matthew 10:37; 19:29 respectively.

31. Matthew 12:48–50.

WEEK THREE: WHAT DOES AN EVERYDAY MISSIONARY DO?

1. Fort Worth facts compiled from U.S. Census Bureau; North Central Texas Council of Governments; Texas State Data Center; Hartford Study on Religion in America; efca.org; Olson, David T. Ten Fascinating Facts about the American Church, CD-ROM (2004), The American Church: www.TheAmericanChurch.org; George Barna, "Church Attendance," The Barna Group, www.barna.org/FlexPage. aspx?Page=Topic&TopicID=10; The Rooted Church, Fort Worth; Fort Worth Star Telegram, "Fort Worth population tops 700,000" (June 26, 2008); Fort Worth Texas Magazine, October 2008.

2. http://fortworthtexas.gov/government/info/default.aspx?id=3252, accessed January 30, 2014.

3. The timeline of Paul's second missionary journey is generally assumed Spring 51–Winter 53. Since he's in Corinth for eighteen months after Athens, many scholars project his stay in Athens to be the winter of AD 51; at most two to three months.

4. Paul Farhi, "Taking Local Coverage to the Limit: 24-Hour Cable News," *Washington Post*, March 11th, 1991, accessed January 30, 2014.

5. This quote from, and following questions summarized from Tim Chester and Steve Timmis, *Everyday Church* (Wheaton, IL: Crossway, 2012), 42–43.

6. These questions from a private document titled "Community Mapping," created by Jonathan Wallace. For related and expanded content, see John Fuder, *Neighborhood Mapping* (Chicago: Moody, 2014).

7. See Luke 10:2–8.

8. See for each: Cornelius: Acts 10; Nicodemus: John 3:1–15; 7:50–51; Gamaliel: Acts 22:3, Acts 5:34–39; Eunuch: Acts 8:26–39. For more on Persons of Peace, see the work of David L. Watson—for example, http://www.davidlwatson.org/2008/03/14/understanding-transition-points—finding-the-person-of-peace/, accessed February 1, 2014.

9. See 1 Thessalonians 2:9; Acts 18:3.

10. See Acts 9:22.

11. See in order below, Matthew 4; Luke 18:29; Romans 16:3; Ezekiel 4:15; various chapters in Acts, especially Acts 2.

12. 1 Timothy 6:18–19 and Acts 2:44–45 respectively.

13. See Luke 16:1–13; quote vv.10, 12.

14. Romans 12:2.

15. Matthew 13:44.

16. See for examples of each: Lost: Psalm 119:176; Matthew 10:6; 18:10. Sinner: Genesis 13:13; Psalm 1:1, 5; Matthew 9:10–13; Luke 6:32–34. Convert: Romans 16:5; 1 Corinthians 16:15; 1 Timothy 3:6. Go after: Luke 15:4. Win their soul: 1 Corinthians 9:22.

17. See many, many examples of each of these activities in the four Gospel accounts.

18. 1 Thessalonians 2:8, NIV, italics added

19. See Acts 8:26–40.

20. John 3:16 and 1 John 4:19 respectively.

21. Andrew Murray, *Experiencing the Holy Spirit* (New Kensington, PA: Whitaker House, 2000), 54.

22. Ibid, 58.

23. John 15:26–27.

24. Previous sentences: John 14:26–27 and John 16: 8, 13–14 respectively.

25. Previous sentences: Matthew 28:20 and Galatians 5:26–26 (specifically vv. 22–23) respectively.

26. Jeremiah 29:7.

27. Murray, 59.

WEEK FOUR: WHEN DOES EVERYDAY MISSION HAPPEN?

1. 1 Corinthians 15:19–20.

2. Previous sentences: 1 Peter 2:13–25; 3:1–7, 8–22 respectively.

3. 1 Peter 2:9.

4. 1 Peter 2:11–12.

5. See Matthew 5:16; also Day 21.

6. For example, see respectively for each bullet below. a) Walking—see the transitions in Mark's gospel: Mark 9:2, 30, 33–34; 10:1, 10, 13, 17, 23, 32, 46; 11:1–2; b) Working:

the multiple passages in the gospel of Jesus healing, miracles, preaching, debating, etc. c) Eating and drinking: Matthew 9:10; 11:19; 14:20–21; 15:37–38; 26:20; Mark 2:16; Luke 24:43; 7:36; 11:37; 14:15; John 13:23–28; the Last Supper passages in each gospel, etc. d) Praying: Matthew 14:23; ch. 26; Mark 1:35; 6:46; 13:33; ch.14; Luke 5:16; 6:12; 9:28+; many public prayers (Matthew 6; John 17; etc.).

7. John 5:19.

8. See Leviticus 10:10 and the chapters following.

9. 1 Corinthians 10:31.

10. Matthew 10:14; Mark 6:11; Luke 9:5.

11. Philippians 2:3–4.

12. Previous sentences: Genesis 16; Numbers 20; Genesis 50 and previous.

13. Previous sentences: Matthew 16; Mark 8; Luke 9, 22.

14. See every Old Testament prophet, and as a few apostolic examples among many, Acts 5–7; 16.

15. Previous sentences: Matthew 25:21, 23; Hebrews 11; Genesis 50:20.

16. 1 Corinthians 3:11.

17. Mark 6:7 and Luke 10:1–2 respectively.

18. Aristotle, "How do you cite something common knowledge?" http://www.quotes.net/quote/38481

19. In order, we see each person's background in Acts 16 (Timothy); 18 (Aquila and Priscilla); 13 (Barnabas); Colossians 4 (Luke); 3 John 1 (Gaius); Acts 16 (Lydia).

20. In order, we see each apostle's background in Matthew 10 (Peter, Andrew, James, and John); Matthew 9 (Matthew); Matthew 10, Luke 6 (Simon); John 1 (Bartholomew, called Nathaniel in John's gospel); John 20 (Thomas); Matthew 4, Mark 3, John 18 (Judas Iscariot).

21. Lesslie Newbegin, *The Gospel in a Pluralist Society* (Grand Rapids: Eerdmans, 1989), 227.

22. Summarized from ibid, 227–33.

23. Philippians 3:20.

24. See Leviticus 23:4–44.

25. Deuteronomy 16:14.

26. See for example, Deuteronomy 16:11; Exodus 23:12.

WEEK FIVE: WHERE DOES EVERYDAY MISSION HAPPEN?

1. Paraphrased from Augustine of Hippo, trans R. Pine-Coffin, *The City of God* (New York: Penguin, 2003).

2. "Dallas Theological Seminary Student Handbook", 4.1.4: http://www.dts.edu/students/studentservices/studenthandbook/, accessed January 17, 2014.

3. Matthew 5:14–16.

4. Tim Chester and Steve Timmis, *Total Church* (Wheaton, IL: Crossway, 2007), 33.

5. See for example, Ecclesiastes 10:19; Psalm 104:15; 1 Timothy 5:23.

6. Acts 10:9–16 NIV.

7. Acts 10:34–35.

8. See Galatians 2:11–14; 6:1–8.

9. See for examples of each: Disciples: Matthew 9:14–17; Mark 2:18–22; Luke 5:33–39. "Wrong people": Mark 2:16; Luke 15:1–7; Matthew 9:10; 11:19; Luke 7:37–38. Rebukes: John 5:1–9; 9:1–16; Mark 1:21–31; 3:1–6; Luke 6:1–5; 13:10–17.

10. Mark Driscoll, *Radical Reformission* (Grand Rapids: Zondervan, 2009), 140.

11. See John 17:15–18.

12. "Humm Vac," *Everybody Loves Raymond*, March 19, 2001.

13. Tim Chester, *A Meal with Jesus* (Wheaton, IL: Crossway, 2012), 19.

14. Scott Bartchy, "Table Fellowship," *Dictionary of Jesus and the Gospels*, ed. Joel P. Green and Scot McNight (Downers Grove, IL: IVP, 1992), 796. Quoted in Chester: *A Meal with Jesus*, 19.

15. See for examples of each: "Tax collectors . . . prostitutes": throughout the Gospels. Peter: Acts 9. Banquet images: Isaiah 25; Luke 9, 14; Revelation 19.

16. Previous sentences: John 1:1–11; Genesis 12:2; Ephesians 1:3.

17. Eugene Peterson, *The Message* (Colorado Springs: NavPress, 2011), 1 Corinthians 13:13.

18. Hebrews 12:2.

19. Caesar Kalinowski: "How to Make Disciples without Adding Anything to Your Life," Austin, TX: Verge Conference, February 2011: http://www.vergenetwork. org/2013/05/28/6-rhythms-to-discipleship-caesar-kalinowski/, accessed September 9, 2013.

20. See for example, Acts 2:42; 1 John 1:3–7; Galatians 2:9.

21. See for example, Deuteronomy 16:11, 14; Leviticus 19:10; Leviticus 19:9; Matthew 19:19; Luke 14:12–14; Mathew 9:10–11; John 13:1–20, respectively.

22. See Romans 16:4; Acts 15:26; Acts 2 and 6, respectively.

23. See Romans 12:7.

24. 1 Peter 4:7–11.

25. Tim Keller, "A Church with an Evangelistic Dynamic," The Gospel-Transformed World (series), New York: Redeemer Presbyterian Church, September 27, 2010, accessed September 10, 2013.

26. John 1:14.

27. See Matthew 16:24–28

28. Alan Hirsch, *The Shaping of Things to Come* (Peabody, MA: Hendrickson Publishers, 2003), 39.

29. To be fair, a few sites have child care for the youngest of the young: kids under eighteen months get to play and have fun together, freeing parents to bless others.

30. See for example, Matthew 10:37; 19:29; Mark 10:29–30; Luke 14:25–29.

31. See for example Scott McConnell, "LifeWay Research Finds Reasons 18- to 22-Year-Olds Drop Out of Church," Lifeway.com, August 7, 2007, http://www.lifeway. com/Article/LifeWay-Research-finds-reasons-18-to-22-year-olds-drop-out-of-church, accessed January 17, 2014, and David Kennaman,. "Six Feasons Young People Leave the Church," *Leadership Journal*: Winter 2012.

32. Matthew 7:9.

33. Proverbs 22:6 and Ephesians 6:4 respectively.

34. Luke 3:7; for the following sentences, see 3:7–14.

35. Shane Barnard and Shane Everett, "Received," *Rocks Won't Cry*, Barnard: 1999.

36. See Matthew 18:14–17.

37. See Hebrews 13:17.

38. Mary and her family now live near Dallas, TX, but this story reflects their time as church planters in southern France. Originally posted at http://www.marydemuth.com/ruin-your-kids-for-the-ordinary-part-1/. Used with permission from the author. For further reading about families on mission, see Helen Lee, *The Missional Mom: Living with Purpose at Home and in the World* (Chicago: Moody, 2010).

WEEK SIX: HOW DO I SHARE THE GOSPEL WITHOUT KILLING THE RELATIONSHIP?

1. See for three examples among many, 1 Corinthians 1:18–25; Luke 3:16–17; 12:49–56.

2. Learn more about Interfaith Youth Core at http://www.ifyc.org.

3. Tim Keller, "A Church With an Evangelistic Dynamic," The Gospel-Transformed World (series), New York: Redeemer Presbyterian Church, September 27, 2010, accessed September 10, 2013; first three bullet points below summarized and adapted from the same.

4. See for a few examples among many, 1 Kings 17; 2 Kings 6; Matthew 7:31–37; John 6:11; Acts 9:40; 28:8.

5. Romans 12:15.

6. See Exodus 17:1–7 and Acts 3:1–10 respectively. See also Moses's interactions with Pharaoh, as well as many of the prophets' and apostles' other miracles.

7. See for examples of each: Obedience: 1 Peter 3:12; 1 John 3:12–22. Reliance: Luke 11:9–13; James 1: 6–8. Display of power: Exodus 32:9–10; Acts 9:40; 1 John 1:9. Surrender: 1 John 5:14–15; Matthew 6:10; 26:39.

8. See for example, Acts 16:13–14; 2 Corinthians 4:6; Galatians 1:15; 1 John 5:14; Romans 8:27.

9. J.I. Packer, "Introductory Essay," in *The Death of Death in the Death of Christ*, by John Owen (London: Banner of Truth, 1988), 4–5

10. "Season 6, episode 24," *MADtv*, May 12, 2001. You can view the hilarious video here: http://www.youtube.com/watch?v=BYLMTvxOaeE.

11. Ephesians 4:14.

12. Ephesians 4:15.

13. If Jeff finally writes a book on this, buy it, and buy copies to give away; it'll rock your world. But until he does, bullets below adapted and summarized (likely inadequately) from Jeff Vanderstelt, "Gospel Fluency," February 18, 2013, http://wearesoma.com/resources/watch/gospel-fluency/, accessed May 25, 2013.

14. Malcolm Gladwell, *Outliers: The Story of Success* (New York: Little, Brown and Company, 2011).

15. Claude Debussy, "Dr. Gradus ad Parnassum," *Children's Corner*, mvt 1, 1908. For solo piano. See a performance here: http://www.youtube.com/watch?v=YxRjk8MxwSs.

16. See Mark 17:14–21.

17. See 1 Samuel 1–3; Acts 15–16; Acts 16–18 respectively.

18. *Braveheart*, Paramount, 1995.

19. Romans 8:23.

END HERE: YOUR MISSION

1. Philippians 2:10–11, italics added.

2. Matthew 9:13.

3. Amos 5:21–24. I first heard this analysis of Amos explained by Matt Carter, "Impure Worship," *Why Churches Die* (series), Austin, TX: Austin Stone Community Church, September 16, 2007.

ACKNOWLEDGMENTS

FROM BEN

Among the many things I've learned in crafting this book, among the most important is what a community effort writing is. Far beyond coauthorship, every person below has made this better than it otherwise would have been, and we're grateful to God for each of you. Thank you, Becky and Jess Connelly, John Mark Day, Ben Disney, Matt Formby, Tina Howard, Billy Patterson, Timm Sasser and Katie Smith—my community of reviewers who spoke into my drafts. Brendan and Betsy Reagan and family, thanks for letting me turn your apartment into a writing cave for weeks on end. Justin Tennison (justintennison.com), thanks for bringing the text to life.

Many thanks to Alan for the foreword, and to Steve, Jeff, Lance, Mark, Mary, and Rick for letting us glimpse into your lives and missions. And there aren't words to thank the Moody crew: Duane Sherman, Betsey Newenhuyse, Parker Hathaway, Erik Peterson, Pam Pugh, and your teams—thank you for giving a rookie writer a chance, answering innumerable questions and serving as sounding boards for hair-brained ideas, and massaging the manuscript so the message rings clear.

Bob Roberts, neither this book nor The City Church would exist without your involvement; I'm deeply grateful for you. To The City Church elders, leaders, and church family: thank you for the time to write, for the sacrifices you made to allow it, and for living your lives and demonstrating the gospel in such a way that fills this book with stories and examples. And to my Jesser, CharlieBear, and MaggieRoo, thank you for grace and patience during this project and my neuroticism, for pursuing this crazy life of everyday mission with me, and for being my girls. I love you.

FROM BOB

People often think of NorthWood as a global church—and it is, but it is even more so a local church because we have a zip code, as Len Sweet would say! Seventy-five percent of the members of NorthWood are involved in some kind of community/neighborhood engagement. The refugee volunteers, the volunteers at the apartment complexes, the downtown Fort Worth volunteers, the volunteers at the Academy of West Birdville, the volunteers at the Senior Center in Haltom City, the volunteers at Nash Elementary, the clinics—and the incredible staff at NorthWood Church that lives, models, connects, and equips it's members to engage like crazy.

I really enjoyed getting to know the Moody team: Duane Sherman, Betsey Newenhuyse, Parker Hathaway, and Erik Peterson. Ben Connelly, so many of us believe in you—run hard, run steady, run long. Stay in the Jesus zone. Thanks for all the contributors for the book: Alan, Steve, Jeff, Lance, Mark, Mary, and Rick. Especially to the global church—be patient, we are coming . . .

FROM BEN AND BOB

We've had the **honor** of learning from many mentors and practitioners over the years—through their writing, formal meetings, and informal conversation. While we noted everyone we knew of, whose words or concepts we recall, it's likely that some of the content was drawn from memory, as their thoughts have since become internalized and part of our own. To anyone left unnamed who has taught us well, we are grateful to God for you, and your wisdom and influence.